OKLAHOMA ORIGINALS

OKLAHOMA ORIGINALS

EARLY HEROES, HEROINES, VILLAINS & VIXENS

JONITA MULLINS

THE
History
PRESS

Published by The History Press
Charleston, SC
www.historypress.com

Cover photographs, author's collection.

First published 2019

Manufactured in the United States

ISBN 9781467143523

Library of Congress Control Number: 2019937040

Contents

INTRODUCTION

The history of the Twin Territories—which became the state of Oklahoma—is peopled with fascinating characters. For many who came here, this place was the end of a difficult and tragic trail. For others, it was a place of new beginnings in a land of opportunity. Whatever their reason for coming to this heartland of America, the people of early Oklahoma were a colorful crew who left an indelible mark on the landscapes and streetscapes of the state.

Sometimes called the "most American state" because of its beautiful diversity of land and people, Oklahoma was settled unlike any other colony or territory. From the forced removal of many native nations and slaves to land runs to outlaws on the run to the migration of "state blacks" looking for opportunity, an array of interesting, colorful and courageous people made Oklahoma their home for a short time or for a lifetime. Here are eighty-four brief biographies of some of those individuals who shaped the state and gave it the unique character and culture it is known for today.

CHAPTER I

THE EXPLORERS

FORT GIBSON OFFICER EXPLORED
THE GREAT AMERICAN WEST

Benjamin Bonneville was born in France in 1796. With his mother and younger brother, he immigrated to America in 1803. His father, Nicolas de Bonneville, was a publisher in France who spoke out for a democratic government. He was jailed for his political views and could not accompany his family to the young United States. But his friendship with Thomas Paine and the Marquis de Lafayette helped his family settle in their new home.

At age seventeen, Benjamin entered the Military Academy at West Point; it is likely that Thomas Paine assisted him in gaining admittance to the school. Bonneville graduated in 1815 as a second lieutenant, and as most new West Point graduates, he was sent to the frontier as one of his early assignments. He served at Fort Smith at a location known as Belle Point in Arkansas Territory.

At Fort Smith, Bonneville was assigned to the Seventh Infantry under Colonel Matthew Arbuckle. In 1824, the government decided to build a fort farther west at a location known as the Three Forks where the Arkansas, Verdigris and Neosho (Grand) Rivers meet. Bonneville was aboard one of the keelboats that brought the first supplies to Cantonment Gibson. He remained at the fort until 1825, when he was given a special assignment.

The renowned Marquis de Lafayette, a hero from the American Revolution, was visiting America, and he requested the young lieutenant accompany him on his tour as his clerk. Lafayette and Bonneville made state visits to former presidents Jefferson, Monroe and Madison and also to the current president, John Quincy Adams. Benjamin even returned to France with Lafayette and spent about ten months there before returning to Fort Gibson in 1826.

Bonneville found Fort Gibson much busier than when he had left, and the stockade had been completed. With the Indian removals expected to become official government policy under President-elect Andrew Jackson, the fort was becoming the center of activities relating to the removals. Bonneville attended a meeting with the Cherokee Council at the home of Chief John Jolly. He also helped survey the road from Fort Smith to Fort Gibson, which would become an important supply route and one part of the Trail of Tears.

Now a captain in the military, Benjamin Bonneville had a keen interest in the exploration of the American West, still shrouded in mystery and myth. Bonneville accompanied several expeditions through western Oklahoma, identifying unknown species of flora and fauna and documenting the tribes

The Bonneville House still stands near downtown in Fort Smith, Arkansas. *Author collection.*

of the Plains. Later, from 1832 to 1835, Bonneville took a leave of absence from Fort Gibson and explored even farther west. He brought back an authentic study of the geography of the region that included the Great Salt Lake of present-day Utah and the presence of oil in Wyoming.

Bonneville turned his study of the American West into a book titled *The Adventures of Captain Bonneville*. Its geographic detail and reliable maps made it a resource for early pioneers striking out to settle the vast reaches of America. His book also created the image of the Mountain Man, an American icon of the early West.

Bonneville returned in 1836 to the army at Fort Gibson, where several companies of Dragoons were now stationed. He remained at Gibson until 1839 but continued in the army for many years, achieving the rank of general. His final assignment was commander of Jefferson Barracks in Missouri. He retired to live in St. Louis and was buried at the Bellefontaine Cemetery there in 1862. His widow built a home in Fort Smith after his death, and it still stands today.

WASHINGTON IRVING IMMORTALIZED
THE PRAIRIES OF OKLAHOMA

In 1832, Congress created a commission to assist in the relocation and settlement of the Five Civilized Tribes in Indian Territory. This commission chose Fort Gibson as its headquarters, it being the westernmost U.S. outpost at that time and located in the heart of the lands being set aside for the Indians.

The commission was also given the task of making treaties with the Plains Tribes who roamed the western sections of the territory following the annual migration of the buffalo. Until this time, many of these tribes had made no treaty with the United States and had had little contact with American settlement.

Three men were appointed to the commission: Montfort Stokes, Reverend John Schermerhorn and Henry Ellsworth of Hartford, Connecticut. Congress put at their disposal the Mounted Ranger Company under the command of Captain Jesse Bean, who would be stationed at Fort Gibson.

Captain Bean arrived at Fort Gibson in September 1832 and was shortly ordered to undertake an exploration of the western regions of the newly established Indian Territory. His mission was to try to make initial contact with the Plains Tribes such as the Comanches and Pawnees.

In the meantime, Henry Ellsworth was traveling westward from Connecticut. Onboard a steamship on Lake Erie, Ellsworth met the famous author Washington Irving, who was interested in touring the West. Ellsworth invited Irving to come along with him to Fort Gibson, and Irving jumped at the opportunity. They continued by steamship down the Ohio River to the Mississippi River and then up to St. Louis, where they visited the Chouteaus, a French family of fur traders, and William Clark of the Lewis and Clark Expedition.

From St. Louis, they traveled to Independence and then started south along the Texas Road. Colonel A.P. Chouteau, who operated a trading post on the Verdigris River at the Three Forks, accompanied the party on this leg of their journey. They arrived at Chouteau's Verdigris Trading Post on October 8, 1832, and continued from there the four miles to Fort Gibson. It was necessary to cross the Grand River by ferry, which was operated by soldiers. Irving noted the whitewashed barracks of the fort in his journal.

At Fort Gibson, the Ellsworth party learned that Captain Bean's Rangers had left just three days earlier on his expedition into the Plains. They wished to join the Rangers in this adventure, so Colonel Matthew Arbuckle, commander at the fort, dispatched two Creeks to find Bean, with instructions to wait until Commissioner Ellsworth could join him.

Ellsworth's group spent the next two days getting outfitted for the trip. They limited their supplies to just what could be carried on their own mounts and a few packhorses. They followed the Arkansas River northwest, traveling through what would become Wagoner, Coweta and Bixby, but saw no towns back then, only the neat, well-stocked farms of Creek families on rich river bottom land.

They joined Bean's Rangers at the Cimarron River and proceeded across the prairie in a wide circle of what is now central Oklahoma. They arrived back at Fort Gibson on November 9, weary but well satisfied with their journey. Washington Irving immortalized this adventure in his book *A Tour on the Prairies*.

ENGLISH BOTANIST EXPLORED OKLAHOMA IN 1819

Thomas Nuttall was an English botanist who came to America to study and explore. The American wilderness was a fascination for the scientific community, and many were eager to discover new species of plants and

A portrait of Thomas Nuttall in later years.

animals. All of the exploration parties that Thomas Jefferson sent into the Louisiana Purchase were scientific, in part because Jefferson himself was a scientist and very much interested in the flora and fauna of this unknown land.

The scientific community in America at the time was centered in Philadelphia, and many leading scientists taught and studied there. It was here that the young botanist named Thomas Nuttall arrived from England in 1808. He was primarily self-taught, but he was intelligent and eager to make a name for himself in the scientific community. He was convinced that exploration of the many unknown species of plants in America would give him that opportunity.

Nuttall plunged into his journeys with the exuberance and ignorance of youth. He was a scientist, not a mountain man, and he was not prepared for taking on these journeys, but he somehow managed to blunder through, collecting plants and keeping very detailed journals about his travels. Here was a scientist journeying along sometimes treacherous waters, and he didn't even know how to swim! He traveled throughout Missouri Territory and learned much about dealing with Native Americans, who fascinated him. He was received by the Indians as a "medicine man" because he sought from them information about the plants they used as medicinals.

The botanist reached the Arkansas River in January 1819. The Arkansas piqued the interest of Nuttall because no botanist had ever ascended this river, which meant he would be the first. He decided he would follow its course all the way to its source.

Nuttall's general habit in making his explorations was to hire a local trapper or resident to act as a guide. He stayed for a time at Arkansas Post, which was an important early settlement at the mouth of the Arkansas. Then he ventured upriver to Fort Smith, where he spent time visiting the military post and the doctor assigned there. He accompanied the military during the spring of 1819 on some of its expeditions into southeastern Oklahoma.

After exploring the Fort Smith area, Nuttall was eager to continue up the Arkansas. He persuaded fur trader Joseph Bogey to allow him to travel with him to his trading post on the Verdigris at the Three Forks and arrived in July 1819.

Nuttall would often leave the rivers and strike out on foot across the prairie. For him, this was the only way to explore, since he was interested in collecting plant specimens. When night fell, he would simply curl up on the ground and go to sleep, often without building a fire. He carried a gun but did not really know how to use it.

Nuttall met a trapper at the Three Forks that he referred to only as Mr. Lee. Lee agreed to take Nuttall farther west on the Arkansas. Because it was late summer, they encountered many harsh conditions, including hostile Indians and a lack of water. Nuttall drank from a scummy pond and became quite ill and almost died out on the Plains. He and Mr. Lee were forced to turn back before reaching his goal of finding the source of the Arkansas in the Rockies.

Nuttall returned to the Three Forks and spent time among the fur-trading community located there, recovering from his illness. It was while staying here that Nuttall predicted that an important city would one day be located at the Three Forks area.

SERGEANT FOR LEWIS AND CLARK FOUND HOME AT THE THREE FORKS

When Meriwether Lewis and William Clark launched their famous expedition in 1804, the entire country waited with expectation to learn what they would discover as they crossed the American continent. The Corps of Discovery, as their expedition came to be called, was made up of military men who had experience in frontier exploration—the frontier of Kentucky. One of the sergeants who proved invaluable on the Lewis and Clark Expedition was Nathaniel Pryor.

We know very little of Pryor's early life except that he was born in Virginia and married around age twenty-three. However, only single men were recruited for the Corps of Discovery, so it is believed that Pryor may have been widowed when Captain Clark asked him to join the expedition. Pryor was recruited at Louisville, Kentucky, in October 1803 and was made a sergeant in charge of the keelboat that carried the bulk of their supplies up the Missouri River.

Pryor traveled across the continent of North America with Lewis and Clark, enduring sickness, hunger, cold and all the other deprivations of the difficult journey. Time and again, the two captains commended Pryor in their journals. When the Corps of Discovery returned to St. Louis, every member of the expedition was hailed as a hero, and parties were thrown in their honor wherever they traveled.

Pryor continued in military service as an ensign in the First U.S. Infantry. He served under General Andrew Jackson at the Battle of New Orleans in the War of 1812. He rose to the rank of captain in the Forty-Fourth Infantry and for the remainder of his life was addressed as Captain Pryor.

In 1816, Pryor entered business with a fur trader named Samuel Richards at the French-American settlement of Arkansas Post, located near the mouth of the Arkansas River. He remained there for a few years and then obtained a license to trade with the Osages at a post on the Verdigris River at the Three Forks, where he associated with Samuel Rutherford.

Here, Captain Pryor married an Osage woman and enjoyed good trade relations with Chief Claremont and his band of Osages. Pryor quickly established himself as a highly respected leader among the American traders who were beginning to populate the Three Forks area. His experience with Lewis and Clark had been valuable training for surviving the wilderness and dealing with the native people.

In 1819, Pryor briefly served as a guide along the Verdigris River for Thomas Nuttall, the English scientist who was researching the flora and fauna of the Indian country. He also helped with the establishment of the Union Mission in 1820 among the Osages on the Grand River.

However, Pryor's friendship with the Osages created some difficulties for him. In 1820, the Osages, under a warrior named Mad Buffalo, clashed with the Western Cherokees, and three Cherokees were killed. The Cherokees vowed revenge and sought Mad Buffalo at Pryor's trading post. Pryor aided Mad Buffalo in escaping, and to retaliate, the Cherokees robbed the trading post of a large number of furs.

In 1827, Pryor's former captain and Indian superintendent, William Clark, appointed him as acting U.S. sub-agent to the Osages. So well respected was Pryor that both Sam Houston and Colonel Matthew Arbuckle at Fort Gibson petitioned to make this a permanent position, and so it was in 1831. Unfortunately, Pryor died shortly afterward at his home on Pryor Creek. The creek and the town of Pryor take their name from this American hero.

CHAPTER 2

THE FUR TRADERS

FUR TRADING FAMILY DOMINATED THE FRONTIER

The Mississippi River served as a corridor of French settlements such as New Orleans and St. Louis when Napoleon Bonaparte sold the river and millions of acres west of it to the United States. The Creole families in these towns resented being handed over to American control with no say in the matter.

To try to improve relations with the now French-Americans, President Thomas Jefferson offered to send four young men from the frontier to the new Military Academy at West Point, New York. One of these young men was Auguste Pierre Chouteau. He graduated in 1806, and though his military career was relatively short, he attained the rank of colonel.

The Chouteau family managed a fur trade empire that spanned the Mississippi and Missouri River basins. Their primary trade partners were the Osages of Missouri. In fact, the Chouteaus turned their trade with the Osages into one of the largest fur-trading outfits in America, rivaling that of John Jacob Astor. And along the way, they established themselves as experts in Indian affairs. It was to the Chouteaus that Lewis and Clark turned for assistance in outfitting their Corps of Discovery in 1804.

When their trade monopoly was threatened in 1802, they began to look southward to the Arkansas River for better trade opportunities. Jean Pierre Chouteau followed the course of the Neosho River to the location of a large salt spring and set up a trading post there. It is said that Chouteau had declared this river "grand," thus giving it its French name. In 1817, his son Colonel A.P. Chouteau moved to this fur-trading post at the Grand Saline.

A.P. built a home here and named it La Saline. Like other members of his family, A.P. Chouteau built in grand style, even developing a horse racetrack for entertaining his Indian neighbors. With his Osage wife, Rosalie, Chouteau enjoyed entertaining other visitors as well, such as Nathaniel Pryor and Washington Irving.

In 1819, Colonel Chouteau bought the fur-trading outfit of Henry Barbour and George Brand. Their post was located just below the falls of the Verdigris River at the Three Forks. Along the Verdigris, a number of other trading posts were engaged in a thriving business. The earliest had been established in late 1806 by Joseph Bogey, and he was followed by other traders such as Nathaniel Pryor, Hugh Glenn and Samuel Rutherford. According to historian Grant Foreman, this fur-trading community was the earliest non-Indian settlement located in what became Oklahoma.

From the Three Forks, Chouteau launched a boat-building business that employed several men. Chouteau would load his keelboats with furs and

The Chouteau Memorial was built at Salina, the town that developed from the Chouteau trading post. *Oklahoma Historical Society.*

transport them to New Orleans, where he would also sell the boat. Then he would return home with a load of trade goods for his many trading posts strung along the Three Rivers.

When Colonel Matthew Arbuckle ascended the Arkansas River in 1824, looking for a site to locate a fort in the Three Forks area, he originally intended to build on the Verdigris River. But he found that the best boat landing on that river was already occupied by this bustling community of fur traders, so the fort was placed on the Grand River instead.

Besides being regarded as an astute businessman, Colonel Chouteau was also a recognized authority in Indian Territory. Until his death in 1838, Chouteau was frequently involved in treaty negotiations among the various Indian tribes. The military at Fort Gibson would often consult with him on matters relating to Native Americans. Officials in Washington often deferred decisions on Indian affairs to him. For three generations, the Chouteaus were one of the most important families on the American frontier.

SAM HOUSTON MADE THE THREE FORKS HOME FOR A SHORT TIME

While no U.S. president has ever called Oklahoma his birthplace, three men who would later serve as president all crossed paths on the frontier of the Three Forks. At the time, the stockade of Fort Gibson, a few trading posts, the Creek Indian Agency and some Creek and Cherokee homesteads were all that made up the Three Forks area.

Arriving to the Three Forks area in 1829 was Sam Houston. Called "The Raven" by his Cherokee friends, Houston had left a rising political career in Tennessee after resigning abruptly from the office of governor in that state. He moved west to escape the scandal of a failed marriage to live among the Cherokees he had grown up with back in Tennessee.

In Indian Territory, Houston married a Cherokee woman he called Diana but whose Cherokee name was either Tiana or Talihina, according to various sources. He established a trading post and home that he named Wigwam Neosho. The site of his trading post was near present-day Okay, and from his home he could watch the riverboat traffic on both the Verdigris and Neosho (Grand) Rivers where they flow into the Arkansas. He surely also noticed the steady stream of settlers traveling southward along the Texas Road that forded the Arkansas River near his home.

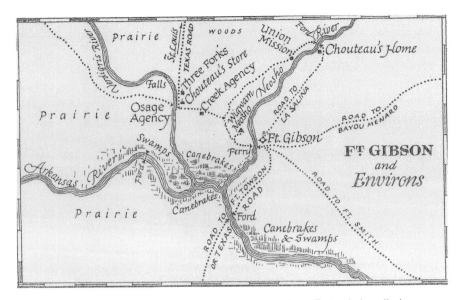

This map shows the location of Sam Houston's home at Three Forks. *Author collection.*

On his arrival in Indian Territory, Houston almost immediately plunged into tribal affairs, often advising the commander at Fort Gibson on dealings with the Indians. His Cherokee friends asked him to travel with their second chief Blackcoat to Washington to address issues of Indian sovereignty.

After working with the Cherokee for three years, Houston left Indian Territory and Diana for a new life in Texas. He later sent for Diana to join him, but she refused, not feeling she would fit in the white world and not wanting to leave her own people.

Houston quickly involved himself in the volatile politics of Texas. Being officially a part of Mexico, the Texas territory was rapidly being settled by Americans who clamored for independence. Houston, who had served in the military during the War of 1812, was appointed general in a growing Texas army.

He served as a delegate to the convention that declared Texas independence in 1836. Houston was promptly named commander of all the Texas forces. Just over a month later, Houston and his men defeated Mexican general Santa Anna at the Battle of San Jacinto, which decisively won Texas independence from Mexico.

In the fall of that same year, Sam Houston was elected first president of the Republic of Texas. He served two terms as president, and the town of

Houston was established as the republic's capital. After Texas joined the Union in 1845, Houston represented the state as a senator.

He fell from political favor, however, because he opposed Texas's secession from the Union to join the Confederacy. Houston was removed from office in 1861 and died just two years later in July 1863. His son Temple Houston was a prominent lawyer in Oklahoma Territory in later years.

SAMUEL RUTHERFORD FAMILY IS ONE OF OKLAHOMA'S OLDEST

The Three Forks area might have been a remote wilderness when it became part of the United States in 1803, but within a decade, it was getting crowded, at least by frontier standards. Like a magnet, the three rivers seemed to pull traders into the region, all hoping to profit from the abundance of fur-bearing animals that inhabited the spring-watered prairie.

One of the traders who came early to this region was Samuel Morton Rutherford, who had been born in Virginia around 1795. At age twelve, he and his family settled in Tennessee, and he completed his schooling there. When he reached seventeen, he joined the Tennessee Volunteers and fought in the Battle of New Orleans in the War of 1812.

That battle against the British to protect the important shipping route along the Mississippi River brought many young soldiers into the Louisiana and Arkansas Territories. Rutherford met another adventurer named Nathaniel Pryor who also fought at New Orleans under General Andrew Jackson. These two young men, probably with many other militiamen mustered out after the war, decided to settle at Arkansas Post and try their hand at the fur trade.

Between 1816 and 1819, Pryor and Rutherford—along with other traders such as Samuel Richards and Robert Mosby French—worked the fur trade between Arkansas Post and the Three Forks. By 1819, Rutherford and French were settled on the west bank of the Verdigris River. According to his great-granddaughter Frances Rosser Brown, Rutherford sold his part of the business to Nathaniel Pryor after just a few years.

Rutherford moved back to Arkansas for a time and quickly moved into positions of authority there. He was sheriff of Clark County and later Pulaski County and served in the Arkansas Territorial Legislature. His experience in trading among the Indians brought him back to Indian Territory when he was appointed a special agent to the Choctaws. He lived at Sculleyville while in this position and also when serving as superintendent of Indian Affairs.

In 1859, he was appointed a member of the commission that would treat with the Seminoles and arrange for their removal from Florida to Indian Territory. Then he stepped into the position of agent to the Seminoles and lived at Wewoka until the Civil War broke out.

In his later years, Rutherford settled at Fort Smith, Arkansas, and was buried at the Oak Cemetery located there. His descendants, however, continued living in the Choctaw Nation of Indian Territory. Brown stated that she believed her family was one of the oldest in Indian Territory because her great-grandfather Samuel Morton Rutherford made the Three Forks his home long before the Indian Removals brought the Five Civilized Tribes to Indian Territory.

SONDHEIMERS LEFT MARK IN INDIAN TERRITORY

Joseph Sondheimer, a Jewish immigrant from Bavaria, arrived in America in 1852 at the age of twelve. He had come to the "land of promise" alone but quickly located family friends in Baltimore and moved in with them. He learned the mercantile trade and tramped about the Midwest as a peddler. He settled in St. Louis, where he opened a hide and fur business just before the Civil War broke out. During the war, he supplied the military at commissary stations along the Mississippi River at locations such as Cairo and Memphis.

In 1866, Sondheimer made a horseback trip through the Indian Territory and liked the potential for trade there. Using his military connections, he opened small trade depots along the military road that ran from Fort Scott, Kansas, to Fort Gibson and on to Jefferson, Texas.

The Three Forks area became his central distribution point because the Texas Road crossed the navigable Arkansas River here. Sondheimer began shipping tons of hides from cattle, buffalo and deer as well as furs, wool and thousands of pounds of pecans to eastern U.S. markets and to Europe.

Traveling on a large white horse, Sondheimer developed a trade circuit throughout the territory, purchasing furs and hides. Unlike other traders in the territory, Sondheimer did not barter for the hides and furs he obtained. He paid the Indians who brought in these goods in gold coin. It is said that he was respected and trusted by the Indians, and though he often carried large amounts of cash while riding through the territory, he was never once robbed.

Eventually, Sondheimer built several large warehouses along the Texas Road where he would store the furs he bought until he could ship them back east. In 1867, Sondheimer built a large warehouse at the Creek Agency at the base of Fern Mountain on the Arkansas River. The Indian agency was a natural choice for a trading location because the Creeks visited there frequently in conducting their business with the government. Soon, other traders were also building around the agency, and a little community developed there.

When the Missouri, Kansas & Texas Railroad established its depot south of the Three Forks in 1872, Joseph Sondheimer and most of the other businesses at Creek Agency moved to the depot site. These businesses formed the core of the new town of Muskogee. Sondheimer's plant was located at the corner of Main and Broadway. Now his furs and pecans were shipped out of the territory by rail.

Sondheimer requested permission to settle in Indian Territory and bring his family there. All this time, Joseph had maintained his residence in St. Louis and simply traveled to his various trading locations by horseback. He had planned to build a home near the old Fort Davis site north of Muskogee because the Missouri, Kansas & Texas Railroad first intended to locate a depot there. When the depot was located farther south and Muskogee was born, Sondheimer moved his wife and two sons to this new town instead.

Sondheimer had fur plants at both ends of Second Street in Muskogee. His business continued in Muskogee until 1942, carried on by his sons Alexander and Samuel.

The Sondheimers were very involved in Muskogee's civic activities and were great supporters of the town. Joseph supported the Beth Ahaba congregation, and a stained-glass window in the temple was inlaid with his name and date of death. Samuel served on the board of directors of the First National Bank. He also invested in the Ozark and Cherokee Central Railroad, First National Bank of Stigler and Citizens Bank in Okmulgee.

But it was Alexander Sondheimer who perhaps left the most lasting legacy to Muskogee. He and his wife, Eudora, were tragically killed in an accident while traveling in Europe in 1923. In their estate, they generously bequeathed funds to several Muskogee institutions, including the YMCA, the YWCA, the Boy Scouts, United Charities (an early version of the United Way), the Presbyterian Church and Beth Ahaba Temple.

The most interesting bequest, however, was one to the Masons. The will set aside a sum of money for a Masonic pilgrimage to Pikes Peak to be made in 1998. Joseph Sondheimer had been Indian Territory's only citizen to make a similar trek to Pikes Peak with the Masons in 1898.

CHAPTER 3

THE SOLDIERS

ARBUCKLE LEFT MORE THAN HIS NAME IN OKLAHOMA

As a career military man, Matthew Arbuckle played an important role in early Indian Territory history. He was born in what is now West Virginia in 1778, entered the army at a young age and served for nearly fifty years at posts throughout the South and West.

Arbuckle was a member of the Third Infantry Regiment when he made lieutenant in 1799 at the age of twenty-one. He was moved to several southern posts during the War of 1812 and had risen to the rank of major during that conflict. By the end of the war, he held the rank of lieutenant colonel and was second in command of his unit under General Andrew Jackson.

He saw action in Georgia and Florida during the Seminole Wars from 1817 to 1820. At Fort Gadsden in Florida, he was promoted to colonel and put in command of the Seventh Infantry. In 1822, he and four companies were transferred to Fort Smith to strengthen the military's presence on the frontier.

At that time, the western Cherokees and the Osages were engaged in a series of minor skirmishes over contested hunting grounds in what is today Oklahoma. The infantry at Fort Smith was too far removed from the conflict to be able to effectively deal with it. So General Winfield Scott made the decision to establish a fort farther west. Matthew Arbuckle was authorized to choose a location for this new fort and to direct the Seventh Infantry in building it.

The Three Forks area had been recommended as a good location for a fort back in 1806, so Arbuckle scouted the area, at first thinking he would build on the Verdigris River at its juncture with the Arkansas. But the thriving fur-trading community occupied this area, so Arbuckle instead chose to build on the Neosho (Grand) River.

Construction of Cantonment Gibson began in 1824. The soldiers had to clear the thick river cane for the fort above a natural rock landing point on the river. Later called Fort Gibson, it served as a primary military outpost in what would come to be known as Indian Territory. Colonel Arbuckle commanded the fort for ten years and oversaw the first arrivals of Indians as they were removed from the Southeast.

He briefly left Fort Gibson in 1834 when Henry Leavenworth took command but was called back in just a few months because of Leavenworth's death. He would remain at Fort Gibson until 1841, and during that time, he

The log stockade of Fort Gibson, constructed under Arbuckle's command, was re-created in the 1930s. *Oklahoma Historical Society.*

worked with the Cherokees, Creeks and Seminoles as they ended their Trail of Tears there.

Later, Arbuckle would look back at his time at Fort Gibson and say proudly that he had kept the peace on the frontier. Though there were occasional intra-tribal conflicts, for the most part Indian Territory remained peaceful while Arbuckle was the ranking officer on the frontier.

In 1848, he was transferred to Baton Rouge and then returned to Fort Smith just as the California gold rush was beginning in 1849. Thousands of gold seekers were passing through Fort Smith on their way west, and Arbuckle undertook the task of ensuring safety along the California Trail, which ran through Indian Territory.

He sent troops to establish an outpost on Wildhorse Creek in western Oklahoma to protect westward travelers. Upon Arbuckle's death in 1851, this post was given the name Fort Arbuckle and the mountains around the post gained the name Arbuckle Mountains, as they are called to this day.

FORT BLUNT NAMED FOR HONEY SPRINGS COMMANDER

Shortly after Confederate forces fired on Fort Sumter in South Carolina, commencing the American Civil War, there was a rush among Union sympathizers to raise military forces. In Kansas, a physician named James G. Blunt was among the first to volunteer. He had practiced medicine in Greeley, Kansas, for several years and was a staunch abolitionist.

He joined the Third Kansas Regiment and was given the rank of lieutenant colonel. This regiment was sent to Fort Scott, Kansas, to defend it against Confederate troops under General Sterling Price. After spending several months in pursuit of Price throughout Kansas and Missouri, Blunt was made a brigadier general and placed in command of Fort Leavenworth.

Blunt was responsible for organizing regiments of Creek, Cherokee and Seminole refugees who had fled Indian Territory to Kansas at the outbreak of hostilities. Utilizing these troops, Blunt sent forces into Indian Territory as far as Tahlequah in 1862, but they returned to Fort Scott rather than remain in the territory.

Blunt then left Fort Leavenworth and personally assumed command of the Indian troops. He would later write of them that they remained on active duty until the end of the war and "did excellent service for the Union cause."

Blunt would lead his troops to battles throughout Missouri and Kansas, including the well-known clashes at Pea Ridge and Prairie Grove.

By 1863, Blunt had also added to his command one of the first African American regiments to fight in the Civil War: the First Kansas Colored Infantry. With success in the Arkansas battles, Blunt was determined to secure Indian Territory for the Union. He ordered a subordinate, Colonel William Phillips, to occupy Fort Gibson. Blunt would join Phillips there with additional troops on July 11, 1863.

By that time, General Blunt's reputation as a bold and disciplined fighter had been well established. Upon his arrival at Fort Gibson, its name was changed to Fort Blunt, though it only was referred to by this name for a brief time.

Blunt learned that Confederate troops were massing at a supply depot called Honey Springs about twenty miles south of Fort Gibson. More reinforcements were expected to arrive from Arkansas. Their intent was to attack Fort Gibson. But as he had done on several other occasions, Blunt decided to strike first before the additional troops could arrive.

Leaving Fort Gibson on July 16, Blunt's forces made the march to Honey Springs overnight. They engaged the Confederate troops under General Douglas Cooper at a point where the Texas Road crossed Elk Creek. With the First Kansas Colored Infantry holding the center of the Union line, the Confederate forces were routed and forced to retreat. Because of the Union victory at Honey Springs, Fort Gibson, or Fort Blunt, was never again seriously threatened by Confederate troops for the remainder of the Civil War.

NATHAN BOONE SURVEYED
CREEK-CHEROKEE BOUNDARY

In 1826, the Creeks signed a treaty agreeing to give up their lands in Georgia and Alabama for lands of their choice in Indian Territory. They sent out an exploring party that determined that the best location was in the rich bottomlands of the Arkansas and Verdigris Rivers. By 1828, nearly two thousand Creeks had arrived in Indian Territory and settled on these chosen lands, putting them into cultivation.

That same year, the United States made a treaty with the Cherokees then living in Arkansas Territory that gave them lands the Creeks had already claimed. As the Cherokees began to move into Indian Territory, there was

This stone in a Muskogee neighborhood marks the Cherokee-Creek boundary surveyed by Boone. *Author collection.*

an immediate dispute over land claims. Both tribes could point to treaties giving the same land to each of them. The Creeks were especially anxious to see the matter settled because they had already invested much effort in improving the land and building their homes on it.

The government established an Indian Affairs Commission, consisting of Henry Ellsworth, Montfort Stokes and John Schermerhorn. They were tasked with reaching a settlement of this land dispute. The three-man commission arrived at Fort Gibson in late 1832 and began to work for a resolution of the conflict.

In February 1833, the United States signed new treaties with the Creeks and the Cherokees setting forth a rough boundary line between the two tribes that ran from the Canadian River at the mouth of the North Fork to the Arkansas River at the mouth of the Grand River.

To develop a more exact boundary line, the government hired a young soldier who had arrived at Fort Gibson in command of a company of Rangers. Captain Nathan Boone, son of the famous woodsman and explorer Daniel Boone, had extensive surveying experience. He was also regarded as every bit the expert woodsman his father was, and he knew the geography of the Southwest as well as any other soldier stationed at the fort.

During March and April 1833, Boone established the boundary between the Creek and Cherokee tribes that still applies today. Beginning on March 28, at the mouth of the North Fork of the Canadian, he planted a cedar post to mark the beginning corner. Then he set stones as mile markers the thirty-eight miles north to a spot on the south bank of the Arkansas River opposite the mouth of the Grand River. This would be where the Port of Muskogee is located today. Boone set a second post here to mark the northern corner of the boundary.

Boone kept a field journal of his survey and noted the type of soil and kinds of trees located at each mile marker. A part of the Boone boundary line serves today as the eastern boundary of Civitan Park on Gibson Street in Muskogee across from the Oklahoma School for the Blind.

THE "COLORED CADET" SERVED IN OKLAHOMA

He was born into slavery in Georgia in 1856 with black, white and Cherokee ancestry. But Henry Flipper never let this early status deter him from accomplishment in his life. His parents, Festus and Isabella Flipper, instilled in all their children a desire and drive to succeed.

During Reconstruction, the Flipper family settled in Atlanta, and Henry was able to attend Atlanta University. In 1873, while still a freshman, Flipper received an appointment from Congressman James Freeman to the Military Academy at West Point. Facing harassment because of his race, he nevertheless became the first black graduate of the academy in 1877.

Flipper was commissioned as a first lieutenant and assigned to the Tenth Cavalry stationed in Indian Territory at Fort Sill. He became the first black officer among the four black regiments known as the Buffalo Soldiers.

While at Fort Sill, Flipper wrote an account of his time at school in a book titled *The Colored Cadet at West Point*. He also left a lasting mark on the landscape of the western outpost. Because he was trained as an engineer, Flipper was assigned the difficult task of finding a solution to the standing water on the post that led to mosquito infestations and regular outbreaks of deadly malaria. He developed a drainage system called "Flipper's Ditch" that to this day controls water and soil erosion in the area and successfully eliminated malaria at Fort Sill. This engineering feat is now listed in the National Register of Historic Places.

Though he was only at Fort Sill for less than two years, he was involved in a number of important endeavors. He was a part of the military escort that brought Chief Quanah Parker with his band of Comanches and Kiowas from the Texas Panhandle to Fort Sill. Flipper also surveyed a road and supervised its construction between Fort Sill and Gainesville, Texas. He also oversaw the development of a telegraph line from Fort Supply in Indian Territory to Fort Elliott in Texas.

To his regret, Flipper was transferred to Fort Elliott in 1879 and subsequently served at three other forts in that state. Though most of his commanding officers found Flipper's work to be exemplary, he faced mistrust and racism from others. In 1881, he was charged with embezzlement of quartermaster funds. He was acquitted of the charge in his court-martial but found guilty of conduct unbecoming an officer. He was discharged in 1882.

Flipper went on to other successes in his life but spent the rest of his years working to clear his name. He worked as an engineer for an oil company in Venezuela and served as an assistant to Interior Secretary Albert Fall in Washington.

Flipper did not live to see it, but his record was finally cleared many years later. The army converted his dismissal to an honorable discharge. President Bill Clinton issued a full pardon of Flipper in 1999.

MILO HENDRICKS WAS A ROUGH RIDER HERO

In the early summer of 1898, the possibility of war loomed over the country. Patriotic fervor was running high, and most folks were wearing red, white and blue ribbons on their lapels. The United States had been attacked in the form of the sinking of the USS *Maine* in a Cuban harbor. A swift response to this attack was being urged on every side and was much discussed by Twin Territory citizens.

After the *Maine* had been destroyed by a mine, President William McKinley sought to create an all-volunteer cavalry unit to send to Cuba. The plan was for this unit to be filled with men from the western territories—Arizona, New Mexico, Oklahoma and Indian Territory.

In Muskogee, Judge John R. Thomas Sr., a federal judge for Indian Territory, was in charge of recruiting two troops. Men were sought for enlistment in the First U.S. Volunteer Cavalry. Captain Allyn K. Capron arrived in Muskogee, and a recruiting office was hastily set up in a vacant building. Quickly, a long line of volunteers formed at the door.

Captain Capron weeded through the many applicants and chose the best that he felt Indian Territory had to offer. Many of the recruits were from Muskogee, but Vinita, Pryor, McAlester and other area towns also contributed soldiers to the cause.

Among the recruits was a young Choctaw man named Milo Hendricks. He was attending Henry Kendall College in Muskogee with plans to graduate in 1901. He was a popular and well-known fellow, for he participated in athletics at the college, sang with the Kendall Quartette and was a member of the cadet corps.

Judge Thomas took an active interest in the recruitments and under his guidance saw Troop L and Troop M embark from Muskogee to a training camp. The recruits met at the Katy Depot, and it seemed like all of Muskogee turned out to see them off. Before the volunteers loaded onto the train to San Antonio, they formed a long line, raised their right hands and pledged to defend their country with courage and honor. A monument was later erected at the Katy Depot to commemorate the occasion when Muskogee sent these first troops to war. That monument now resides at the war memorial near the USS *Batfish* at the Port of Muskogee.

Once in San Antonio, the First U.S. Volunteer Cavalry—its official name—quickly became known as Theodore Roosevelt's Rough Riders. After weeks of intense training, they shipped out to Cuba from Tampa, Florida. Anxious

The Kendall College football team gathers on the porch of the college president's home. Hendricks is seated on the top step, third from the right. *Author collection.*

families back home watched the progress of the troops closely, concern for Milo Hendricks and other local soldiers felt by everyone.

On June 24, 1898, the Rough Riders took part in the Battle of Las Guasimas. Besides the Rough Riders, the Tenth Cavalry, the all-black unit known as the Buffalo Soldiers and a regular cavalry unit were present at Las Guasimas. Shortly afterward, they again participated in the Battle of San Juan Hill.

Within a few months, the war was ended and the soldiers were returning home, many sick from malaria and other fevers contracted in the tropical climate. Milo Hendricks did not return home. He was killed at the battle for San Juan Hill and became one of Muskogee's first heroes and casualties of war.

Chapter 4

The Missionaries

PROFESSOR BACONE WAS A PIONEER EDUCATOR

In 1878, a young New Yorker named Almon Bacone came west to Tahlequah to teach religion in the Cherokee Male Seminary. After a year and a half teaching in the national school, Bacone had come to the conclusion that the Indian nations needed native teachers and preachers who could take education and the gospel to their own tribes, in their own language.

Bacone decided to start Indian University, a school that would be open to students from all tribes. He began the school in February 1880 at the Baptist Mission Home (now known as the Bacone Home) in Tahlequah. He started with three students, but by the end of his first term, he had an enrollment of twelve. After a year, the school had two teachers and fifty-six students and had outgrown its location. A larger facility to accommodate the growing student enrollment became necessary.

So Bacone and two Baptist ministers working in Indian Territory—Joseph S. Murrow and Daniel Rogers—approached the Muscogee (Creek) Council about locating the school in the Creek Nation. At first the Creeks showed no interest in such a school, but through the persistence of these three ministers, the Creek Council finally agreed to offer 160 acres near Muskogee for a new Indian University campus.

Rockefeller Hall was the first building on the Muskogee campus, completed in the spring of 1885. It was built with a donation of $10,000

Students and staff of Indian University stand before Rockefeller Hall on campus. Bacone holds the hand of a little girl. *Author collection.*

from noted philanthropist John D. Rockefeller. "Old Rock," as the building was called, housed the classrooms, dormitory, dining hall, teachers' quarters and administration offices. One early student said the three-story building was the largest he had ever seen in his life.

With the help of his students, Bacone packed up the school's books and furnishings in wagons and moved everything from Tahlequah to Muskogee. Jokingly calling it the "Great Removal," the journey of thirty miles was an all-day undertaking.

Professor Bacone was greatly admired by all the students at Indian University. They called his white beard "Uncle Sam" whiskers but held the lay minister in the highest respect. Though not a tall man, when he drew himself up to lecture his students on discipline and faith, they were held silent by the power of his personality.

At his death, Almon Bacone was buried in a small cemetery on the college campus. His tombstone reads, in part: "Hundreds of Indian youth were inspired to a higher life by him." The university changed its name to Bacone College in 1910 in honor of the Baptist missionary who had believed so much in Indian education that he stepped out on faith and built his dream.

CIRCUIT RIDING PREACHER HAD LONG YEARS OF MINISTRY

Reverend M.L. Butler was a Methodist minister who worked in Indian Territory and Oklahoma for over fifty-five years. He was born in Mississippi just before the outset of the Civil War, and his earliest memories were of the horrors of that war and the hardship that followed. They made a lasting impression on him.

When he was twelve, his family moved to Fort Smith, Arkansas. His family lacked the finances for his education, so Butler worked his way through college. Those early years of hard work would prepare him for his later efforts in the ministry. At the age of nineteen, he was licensed to preach in the Arkansas Conference of the Methodist Church.

The following year, he responded to a call for young ministers to work in the Indian Mission Conference in Indian Territory. He arrived at Fort Gibson in 1880 and was assigned a circuit that was seventy-five miles long in the Cherokee Nation. Butler would travel by horseback between churches in the Flint District. He said later in an interview that he often would sleep out on the open prairie but was never once accosted by an outlaw even though his circuit was among the hills notorious for being a gang hideout. He described the land at the time as having grasses that grew seven feet tall and deer and prairie chickens could be seen by the hundreds.

Reverend Butler pastored churches in Fort Gibson, Tahlequah, Okmulgee and Muskogee, among other towns around Indian Territory. During his ministry, he built fifteen churches, married over 1,600 couples and conducted over 2,400 funerals.

He liked to tell the story about conducting a brush arbor meeting in the Chickasaw Nation. One evening after the service had begun, a group of cowboys rode up to the open-air tabernacle and commenced to firing their guns and threatening the preacher. The crowd quickly scattered, and it appeared the revival meeting would not be allowed to continue. But the following day, a group of leading Chickasaw citizens visited the camp of these ruffians. With their own guns in evidence, they informed the cowboys they would be attending the church meeting that night. The cowboys could hardly refuse under the circumstances and did sit quietly in the service that evening. Butler reported that in time, they became "among the best friends of the missionaries."

Butler preached his last sermon to the Indian Mission Conference in Okmulgee in 1937 at the age of seventy-seven. Though he had retired from active ministry, he continued to work for the church until his death in 1938.

MURROW LEFT HIS MARK AT MANY SPOTS AROUND THE TERRITORY

Reverend Joseph Murrow.
Oklahoma Heritage Association.

It is said that hardly a groundbreaking or the laying of a cornerstone could occur in Indian Territory without the presence of Reverend Joseph S. Murrow. As grand master of the Masons, he participated in the ceremony that laid the cornerstone of the Union Agency on August 18, 1875. This cornerstone, still in place at the Five Civilized Tribes Museum, was the first to be laid by the Masons in Oklahoma. Many others are probably scattered throughout the area.

Reverend Murrow was born in Georgia in 1835. He came to Indian Territory at the age of twenty-one, in answer to a call for missionaries to the Native Americans. He worked in the Creek Nation and also the Choctaw Nation and continued in ministry until his death at the age of ninety-four in 1929.

He was one of only a few missionaries who remained in Indian Territory during the Civil War. A tall man who in later years wore a long white beard, Murrow always struggled financially, but he was generous with those he came to serve.

Murrow was especially interested in young people and was very supportive of educational opportunities for Indian youth. He worked with Reverend Almon Bacone when he was searching for a location for his Indian University. Reverend Murrow accompanied Bacone in approaching the Creek Nation with a request for a donation of land near Muskogee for the school.

There is a carved stone Bible on the Bacone College campus that marks the spot where Reverends Bacone, Murrow and Daniel Rogers, a fellow minister, knelt to dedicate the land for the school. Murrow continued to support the school as it grew.

Murrow's mentor in working among the Indians was Reverend H.F. Buckner. It was Buckner who had appealed to Murrow to come to Indian Territory. Buckner operated an orphanage in Dallas, and Murrow spent time there learning about the facility. His concern for Indian youth and determination to protect the interests of those who were disadvantaged by poverty or a lack of education led him to open an orphanage.

He started the orphans' home in Atoka in 1902 but moved it to the Bacone College campus in 1910. The Murrow Indian Children's Home continues the missionary's work even today.

MISSIONARY WAS MASTER LINGUIST

Ann Eliza Worcester was the daughter of Samuel and Ann Worcester, who were serving as missionaries to the Cherokees at Brainerd Mission in Tennessee when she was born in 1826. It was at Brainerd that Ann Eliza first developed a passion for teaching and concern for Native Americans. She, with the Cherokees, made the difficult journey to Indian Territory with her parents when she was just nine years old. The Worcesters continued their work at a new mission at Park Hill near Tahlequah.

Ann Eliza attended the school at Park Hill that her father established. This school would later develop into the Cherokee Female Seminary. The Worcesters were firm believers in education, including for women. Ann Eliza was sent to live with an uncle in Vermont when she was fifteen so that she might pursue a college education at St. Johnsbury Academy.

While most young ladies of that day studied the arts, Ann Eliza studied Greek and Latin, the languages of science. A professor at the school recognized her gift for language and persuaded Ann Eliza's uncle to allow her to pursue this unusual course of study for a young woman.

Ann Eliza returned to Park Hill in 1846 and began work there as a teacher. Though she was a candidate for a master's degree, she felt she was needed at the mission in Indian Territory.

A few years later, she attended a missions conference in Arkansas with her father and there met another young missionary named William Robertson. He was just beginning to work among the Creeks at the Tullahassee Mission. The two young teachers began a courtship, and William would often ride his horse over to Park Hill to visit Ann Eliza there. In 1850, William and Ann Eliza married, and she became his assistant at Tullahassee.

Because she struggled with poor health, Ann Eliza was often bedridden at the mission. Her older daughters, Augusta and Alice, learned at a very young age to shoulder the responsibility of caring for their younger siblings

Translator Ann Eliza Worcester Robertson. *Oklahoma Historical Society.*

and helping run the mission. Altogether, Ann Eliza bore seven children, but three died at young ages.

Despite her illness, Ann Eliza worked even from her bed. Her gift for languages made her a capable translator, and the hours she spent resting were also spent translating the Bible, hymns and school primers into the Muscogee language.

Ann Eliza used her adversity as an opportunity, and for the remainder of her life, she was faithfully working on a translation. In early Muskogee city directories, Ann Eliza Robertson's occupation was listed as "translator." In her lifetime, she translated the entire New Testament from Greek into Muscogee.

Her work earned her the respect of the mission community. In 1892, she was awarded an honorary doctorate from the University of Wooster in Ohio. She was the first woman in the United States to receive such an honor.

In later years, Ann Eliza lived with her daughter Alice in Muskogee, where she continued her translation work and served as professor emeritus for Henry Kendall College. She was not able to lecture at the college but was always willing to tutor young students who needed her assistance. Always a missionary at heart, Ann Eliza died at age seventy-nine in 1905 and was working on the fifth revision of her New Testament translation at the time of her death.

Chapter 5

Law Enforcement

LIKE OTHERS, CANTON LIVED ON BOTH SIDES OF THE LAW

He was born Josiah Horner in 1849. While he was young, "Joe" moved with his family to Texas and developed his skills as a cowboy, trailing herds through Indian Territory into Kansas after the Civil War. But in 1871 at age twenty-two, he fell into a bad crowd and began rustling cattle and robbing banks. It made him a wanted man.

By 1874, he was being pursued by the law and on the frontier that included the soldiers who manned the western forts. At one point, he engaged in a gun battle with a group of Buffalo Soldiers, killing one and wounding another. With a price on his head, Horner was captured by Texas Rangers but managed to escape and fled to Nebraska.

Now away from the negative influences of his youth, Horner vowed to change his ways. He also chose to change his name because he was still a wanted outlaw. He became Frank Canton and lived the rest of his days under that name, trying to atone for his earlier crimes.

He moved to Wyoming and worked on the big cattle ranches there. Soon, he was hired as a detective by the Wyoming Stock Growers Association. He then was elected sheriff of Johnson County, Wyoming, in 1882, and during this time of service, he married and had two children.

When a range war broke out in Johnson County in 1892, Canton was serving as a U.S. deputy marshal and was caught in the middle of it. Regretful

Adjutant General Frank Canton. *Oklahoma Historical Society.*

over the death of a friend and lynching of a woman, Canton moved his family to Oklahoma Territory in 1894.

He settled in the Pawnee area and went to work for Judge Isaac Parker and the Fort Smith court. He served with other marshals such as Heck Thomas and Bass Reeves, making enemies of outlaws while working to clean up the Twin Territories.

One such outlaw was Bill Dunn, whom Canton had arrested for cattle rustling. Once out of prison, Dunn vowed to kill Canton. He accosted the deputy marshal outside the Pawnee courthouse in 1896. The rustler reached for his gun, but Canton was faster and shot the man in the street. The killing was ruled self-defense.

At Oklahoma statehood, Governor Charles Haskell appointed Canton adjutant general of the National Guard, and he spent the next decade building the unit from the ground up. Sometime during this period, Canton met the governor of Texas. He quietly confessed to the man about his crimes in Texas from decades earlier. The Texas governor took into account Canton's years of law enforcement service and issued a pardon for Josiah Horner.

Even so, the lawman chose to keep the name Frank Canton, and this he took to his grave when he died in 1927. He was buried in Edmond, and his grave marker bore the name of a reformed man who had done his best to atone for his life on the other side of the law.

GRIMES CREDITED WITH FORMATION OF OKLAHOMA LAW ENFORCEMENT

William Grimes was born in Ohio in 1857 but moved to Nebraska as a young man. There he worked as a newspaperman and later served as a county sheriff, gaining valuable law enforcement experience. Grimes participated in the 1889 land run in Indian Territory and settled on a farm near Kingfisher.

Grimes quickly moved into real estate and built some of Kingfisher's business and residential neighborhoods. He played a role in establishing Kingfisher College and was active in Republican politics. In 1892, he helped to build the Kingfisher County Courthouse.

When Oklahoma Territory was established in 1890, Grimes was appointed U.S. marshal for the territory. In this role, he faced the enormous task of setting up a law enforcement system where none had existed. Lawlessness was a problem in the territory, so Grimes employed between fifty and one hundred deputy marshals during his years in office. These marshals included such notable men as Heck Thomas and Bill Tilghman.

Grimes served as marshal for only three years but left a lasting mark on the office. He set up a record-keeping system and established courtrooms and jails across Oklahoma Territory. His excellent managerial skills did not go unnoticed.

In 1901, Grimes was named the territorial secretary under Governor William Jenkins. The governor was soon embroiled in a controversy, however, over a questionable government contract. When Jenkins was removed from office, Grimes served as acting governor for about ten days until Thomas Ferguson assumed the governorship. Grimes then served in Ferguson's administration until 1906.

The "ten-day governor" had served for several years as the chair of the Territorial Republican Committee and as a delegate to the National Committee. After Oklahoma's statehood, however, Grimes and his family moved west, settling first in Oregon and then California.

DEPUTY MARSHAL BUILT HIS REPUTATION
ON INTEGRITY

Before the Emancipation Proclamation freed slaves in the South, the Creek Nation was apparently a known safe haven for escaping slaves from nearby states. According to oral tradition handed down among freedmen descendants, Creek leaders refused to allow bounty hunters to enter their nation to capture escaped slaves. Nor would they return such individuals found within their borders.

This may be why an escaped slave named Bass Reeves made his way from Texas and spent a few years living in the Creek Nation. While hiding in Indian Territory, Reeves learned the Muscogee language and the lay of the land.

Following emancipation, Reeves settled on a farm near Van Buren, Arkansas, married and started a family. From time to time, he earned extra money acting as a scout and tracker for lawmen working in Indian Territory.

After the Civil War, Indian Territory had become a haven for criminals fleeing federal jurisdiction. In 1875, the federal court in Van Buren (later moved to Fort Smith) was given jurisdiction over Indian Territory.

Judge Isaac Parker was determined to clean up the region and recruited Bass Reeves and nearly two hundred other men as deputy U.S. marshals. Parker had particularly sought African Americans for the service, and it is believed Bass Reeves was one of the first black deputy marshals to be sworn to duty west of the Mississippi.

Reeves quickly established his reputation as a fearless lawman whose quick draw saved his life on many occasions. Known for his courteous manners and strict sense of duty, the marshal spent thirty-two years in the service and was responsible for nearly three thousand arrests.

After a federal court was established in Muskogee in 1889, Reeves moved to Indian Territory and took up residence for a time in quarters near the federal jail. Along with other marshals such as Bud Ledbetter, Reeves often found his duties involved enforcing the law that made it a crime to produce or sell alcohol in Indian Territory. Though the territory had been "dry" for years, the illegal sale of alcohol had always existed. "Busting" up stills and arresting those who brought whiskey into the Indian nations kept the federal marshals busy.

Bass Reeves was dogged in his determination to end the bootlegging that went on in Indian Territory. In fact, it was probably here that the term "bootleg" whiskey began. Moonshiners would slip the thin flasks of alcohol into the legs of their boots to bring it into the Indian nations.

A group of Muskogee police officers with Bass Reeves at left in the front row. *Author collection.*

Reeves continued as a deputy marshal until Oklahoma statehood in 1907. At that time, he went to work for the Muskogee Police Department. Even at age sixty-nine, his reputation as a lawman was so intimidating that crime was nonexistent on his police beat.

Bass Reeves died in 1910 and was lauded in memorials as one of the greatest lawmen to have served in Indian Territory and one of the greatest U.S. deputy marshals in their more than two hundred years of service.

DAUGHTERS FOLLOWED FATHER INTO LAW ENFORCEMENT

William Grant Rogers was born in the Cherokee Nation in 1865, a member of the influential Rogers and Fields families among the Cherokees. His father, Hillard Rogers, was born in Georgia, removed with his family to Indian Territory and later served as an interpreter for General Zachary Taylor during the Mexican War. His mother was Martha Fields, who had come to Indian Territory with her parents from Tennessee.

After the Civil War, the Rogers family settled on the Caney River when William was still a baby, and Hillard went into ranching. Tragically, William lost both his parents in 1871 within eight months of each other. He was taken in by Nelson Carr, a family friend, and attended school at the Cherokee Orphan Asylum at Salina.

It was at Salina that William met Lillie Washington, also a Cherokee orphan whose parents died while she was quite young. The two married in 1891 and settled near Dewey, where William also farmed and raised stock on an eighty-acre tract of land. Rogers was appointed a U.S. deputy marshal serving the federal courts at Fort Smith and then Muskogee. William and Lillie had seven children, three daughters and four sons.

It was the two oldest daughters who followed their father into law enforcement. Lula, born in 1893, and Rilla Blanche, born in 1895, had their father's sense of adventure and a passion for keeping the peace. Both young women were commissioned as deputy marshals in 1913 at Dewey, Oklahoma. At the time, they were the only women in the state to hold office in law enforcement.

Their commission was not without criticism. Some wondered if young women should be allowed to risk their lives against the criminal element. The young ladies responded that if they were willing to take the risk, why should anyone else worry?

The Rogers sisters were commended in the press for their bravery and valor. They were particularly effective at enforcing Oklahoma's liquor laws and made over fifty arrests during their brief careers. Said to be as

Deputy Lula Rogers. *Author collection.*

skilled as soldiers with a gun, the young women proved valuable in fighting the "introduction" of liquor into the state because they could search women who would sometimes hide flasks in pockets sewn into their petticoats.

Though they were commissioned in 1913, Lula and Blanche had ridden with their father before that. They would often accompany him when he was on duty scouting for bootleggers along the "booze trail" out of Kansas.

One story is told about Blanche riding in a wagon with her father near Caney. They encountered a couple of bootleggers hauling "stock" in a wagon of their own. Before her father could pull his rifle from its scabbard, Blanche had reached for a pistol kept under the seat. She had a drop on the men before they knew what had happened. Father and daughter then hauled the men and their cargo to jail.

Though they had the full support of their neighbors in Dewey, the Rogers sisters were not reappointed as deputies when a new marshal took office a few years later. But their courageous exploits gained them many fans and supporters among the suffragettes of the era, who saw the Rogers sisters as examples of what women could accomplish when they stepped into nontraditional roles for women.

LAWMAN SAM SIXKILLER BROUGHT ORDER TO TERRITORY

Before a federal court was located in Muskogee for Indian Territory, the Union agent to the Five Civilized Tribes was the highest federal authority in the Territory. The Indian agent had the authority to make arrests and have miscreants removed from the territory. He also could mediate civil disputes between U.S. citizens and tribal members.

In 1885, Robert Owen became the Union agent and set out to control the lawlessness that plagued the citizens of the Indian Nations. Owen developed a police force that was led by a highly respected lawman named Samuel Sixkiller. As captain of the U.S. Indian Police, Sixkiller is credited with bringing law and order to the Three Forks region. One of his most notable actions was to face the outlaw Dick Glass in a shootout where Sixkiller ended Glass's career as a horse thief and whiskey runner.

In the fall of 1886, Sixkiller was involved in another shootout, this time on Main Street in Muskogee. A group of young ruffians known for smuggling whiskey faced Sixkiller and several deputies. Muskogee citizens ducked for cover as the gunfire began. When the smoke cleared, one deputy had been killed and Sixkiller was slightly wounded. Members of the gang who were left standing fled the scene, and a posse later gave chase to them.

Sixkiller recognized that the unregulated flow of whiskey was behind much of the lawlessness of the territory, and he became relentless in tracking down the illegal caches of alcohol. One story is told about Captain Sixkiller finding bottles of the homemade brew stashed within the hollowed-out logs of a bootlegger's cabin.

Unfortunately, Sixkiller's diligence in upholding the law did make him many enemies and the target of those who held a grudge against him. On Christmas Eve 1886, horse races were being held at the fairgrounds and whiskey was flowing freely among the crowd of onlookers. Two men came into Muskogee, thoroughly drunk and looking for trouble. Stealing weapons from constable Shelly Keys and a guest at the Mitchell House Hotel, they began to roam the streets of Muskogee.

Coming to the Turner and Byrne Hardware, they saw Captain Sixkiller as he stepped out onto the wooden porch. Being connected with the earlier shootout in the fall, the two men turned their guns on the police captain. Sixkiller was unarmed, having stopped at the mercantile to buy Christmas gifts for his children. The outlaws fired several shots, and Sixkiller fell dead on the steps of the store.

Samuel Sixkiller's funeral was one of the largest ever held at the Rock Church on Cherokee Street in Muskogee. People from all over the territory came to pay their respects to a brave lawman who had done more than almost anyone in bringing peace and security to the territory.

Chapter 6

THE OUTLAWS

GIRL OUTLAWS THE STUFF OF LEGENDS

With other famous female outlaws, more myth than truth often surrounds their stories. This is certainly true of two young women who gained the nicknames Cattle Annie and Little Britches. They were still in their young teens when they were arrested and sent to prison back east.

Little is known about the diminutive girl called Little Britches other than her real name of Jennie Midkiff. A sidekick to Anna McDoulet, Jennie was reportedly a feisty girl who preferred wearing britches instead of skirts.

Anna, or Annie, as she was called, came from a respectable family. Her father was a judge who had begun his law practice in Kentucky. He settled his family in Kansas, where Annie was born in 1882, and then moved to Red Rock, Indian Territory, when Annie was twelve. There her father served as a justice of the peace.

There is no record of either girl receiving much education. Annie worked at odd jobs such as a dishwasher at a restaurant and as a domestic. At some point shortly after the McDoulet family moved to Indian Territory, the two girls must have met and become friends.

Reportedly, the girls were fascinated with the dime novels of the day, which romanticized the outlaw life and likely inspired them to embark on their own brief crime spree. Legend says they were horse thieves and spies for such gangs as the Daltons and Doolins, but it is highly unlikely that such tales are true. They were, however, not afraid to carry guns, and some reports suggest they knew how to use them.

The girls were arrested for selling liquor on the nearby Otoe and Osage reservations. It is possible that they stole the alcohol that they were selling, perhaps from the restaurant where Annie worked. The arrest of the girls is attributed to deputy marshals Steve Burke and Frank Canton.

Convicted of their crime, Annie, at age thirteen, and Jennie, who was probably even younger, were sent to a girls' reformatory in Framingham, Massachusetts. After their release, Annie worked for a time in Massachusetts as a domestic. Jennie is said to have returned to Indian Territory and settled in Tulsa, where she eventually married and lived a quiet, law-abiding life.

In time, Annie also returned, settling in Perry, Oklahoma Territory. She married twice and joined a Wild West show for a time but eventually lived with her second husband, William Roach, in Oklahoma City. There she took work as a bookkeeper and lived a long life, active in the American Legion Auxiliary and the Olivet Baptist Church.

BOOMER LEADER DID NOT GET HIS CLAIM

William Couch was born in North Carolina in 1850 to Meshach and Mary Couch. Following the Civil War, the Couch family settled in Kansas. William had few opportunities for an education, but he was well-read and self-taught. He married Cynthia Gordon in 1871, and they set up their household on a farm near Douglass, Kansas. When the rail line extended to Wichita, they moved to that town.

Couch operated a number of businesses in Wichita, including a grain elevator and grocery store. But tough economic times caused him to lose much of his wealth. Only his livestock business helped the family survive the downturn.

In 1879, Couch heard a lecture given by David L. Payne, a Kansas politician who had taken up the cause of opening the unassigned lands in the center of Indian Territory. Couch became a disciple of Payne and financially supported his "Boomer movement." Repeatedly, Payne led his "Oklahoma Colony" into the unassigned lands to illegally squat on Indian land. Each time, the U.S. Army, often the Buffalo Soldiers, were sent from Fort Reno to escort them back to Kansas.

Boomer leader William
Couch. *Oklahoma Historical
Society*.

After Payne's death in 1884, Couch was elected to lead the Boomers. He had already taken two expeditions into the Oklahoma country. Both efforts had ended with the colonists being forced to return home. Couch, like Payne before him, was arrested for his clear violation of the law.

The Boomers continued to press their case to Kansas politicians, and after another four years, Congress approved the Oklahoma Bill in February 1889. The president signed the law and set the time for the land run at noon on April 22. A clause in the law stated that no one could make a claim earlier than this date and time.

But Couch had defied the law repeatedly, so this "sooner clause" did not stop him. With his father and brothers, he formed the Seminole Surveying Company even though he had no surveying experience. The government had authorized surveys to be made before the land run to facilitate the claims of town lots. After the surveys were completed, the workers were to leave the unassigned lands and wait with everyone else to make a claim.

The Couches remained, however, pretending to be railroad workers. At noon, they simply walked to the claims they wanted and marked eight tracts of prime land in what would become Oklahoma City. Thousands of land disputes made their way through the courts in the following years. Ultimately, the tract William Couch had staked a claim to was awarded to another settler named Robert Higgins. Couch was shot in a dispute over the property and died of his wound in April 1890. Like many other "sooners," Couch never received the land claim that he might have if he had simply obeyed the law.

WYATT EARP WAS ARRESTED IN INDIAN TERRITORY

Wyatt Earp is probably best remembered for his part in the shootout at the OK Corral in Tombstone, Arizona, in 1881. But before that, Earp had a long and checkered career on both sides of the law. Earp entered law enforcement when he served as town marshal of Lamar, Missouri, in 1870. From 1871 to 1873, he roamed the southern plains between Kansas and Texas working as a buffalo hunter.

According to a grand jury indictment handed down in Fort Smith, Arkansas, in April 1871, Wyatt Earp and two other men named Edward Kennedy and John Shown were accused of stealing horses in Indian Territory. The theft allegedly occurred on March 28, 1871, somewhere in the Three Forks area near Fort Gibson. Two horses were taken from the corral of Jim and William Keys.

Deputy U.S. marshal J.G. Owens of Fort Smith obtained a warrant for the arrest of the three men. He set out with a posse made up of Hiram Keys, George Francis, James Jones and Nelson Flousburg to scour the Cherokee Nation for the wanted men. Earp, Kennedy and Shown were arrested for horse theft on April 13, 1871.

Meanwhile, in Fort Smith, Anna Shown, wife of John Shown, was giving a sworn statement that same day to U.S. commissioner James O'Churchill. She told the court that Earp and Kennedy had gotten her husband drunk and then they stole the horses from Jim and William Keys. Shown was given charge of the horses and told to ride north fifty miles, where Earp and Kennedy would meet up with him.

According to Anna Shown, she traveled with Earp and Kennedy in a hack to meet her husband at the designated spot. Then Earp traded out the two horses pulling their hack for the two stolen horses. Wyatt continued on toward Kansas with the stolen horses. Anna, John and Edward followed at a slower pace, traveling at night and sleeping during the day.

Three nights after the theft, Jim Keys caught up with the Showns and Kennedy at about three o'clock in the morning. Shown offered Keys the two horses they had, even though they were not the ones stolen from him. Kennedy told Keys that John Shown was the one responsible for the theft. Anna stated that Earp and Kennedy had threatened her husband to keep him silent about what actually took place.

Apparently, all three men accused of the theft never made it to Kansas, for their arrest took place in the Cherokee Nation. They were taken to Fort Smith, where they appeared before a judge and bail was set at $1,500 for each of them. The fate of the three is unclear after this. A notation on the back of their arrest warrant indicates that a jury acquittal had occurred, but it isn't clear if all three men were tried and acquitted or just one.

Whatever the case, the law did not continue to pursue Wyatt Earp for his involvement in the incident. He went on to serve on the police forces of Ellsworth, Wichita and Dodge City, Kansas, through most of the 1870s before moving to Arizona. Before his troubles at the OK Corral, Earp created some trouble of his own at a corral near Okay.

TRAIN ROBBERY BROUGHT FAMOUS OUTLAW AND LAWMAN TOGETHER

Train robberies were a common problem in Indian Territory beginning as early as 1871 when the first railroad entered the Indian lands. The general lawlessness of the territory following the Civil War made trains particularly vulnerable to the gangs who roamed the region.

The Missouri, Kansas & Texas Railroad (the Katy), because of its route through Indian Territory, was one of the most targeted rail lines in the country. It passed through large stretches of sparsely inhabited land, which made it easy to rob. Gangs began targeting the Katy shortly after it laid the first tracks into the Cherokee Nation.

In response to this constant threat, the railroad hired lawmen to ride the rail line, particularly if a large shipment of money or goods was being transported. In 1894, Bud Ledbetter was hired by an express company to police the railroad. He was on the Katy in mid-November of that year when one of the more famous train robberies occurred.

The year 1894 had seen a great deal of outlaw activity. It was during this time that the U.S. government made a large payment to Cherokee citizens for the purchase of the Cherokee Strip—a northern section of land along the Kansas border. With so much money being transported and changing hands, bandits saw an opportunity for easy spoils.

Such rich pickings attracted an outlaw known as "Texas Jack" to Indian Territory. This outlaw, whose given name was Nathaniel Reed, had spent most of his adult life robbing banks and stagecoaches in Texas, Missouri and Colorado. Though he never killed anyone, he was not averse to carrying an arsenal of guns and threatening their use in his many robberies.

Texas Jack and Bud Ledbetter were destined to meet when Reed attempted to rob the Katy Flyer on the night of November 13. Ledbetter and three other law officers were riding the train that night. The Katy had boarded passengers in Muskogee on the northbound train. There was an express car, carrying money no doubt, plus three passenger cars and a sleeper.

It was a common practice among would-be train robbers to "switch" a train to a side rail at some dark and isolated location. About eight miles north of Muskogee, near the community of Wybark, was the Blackstone Switch. Here was where Texas Jack attempted to waylay the Katy Flyer.

However, the alert engineer saw the switch turn from red to green and recognized what was happening. He set the brake to slow the train down and then threw it into reverse, causing the train to stop short of where Jack and his gang waited. It also threw the passengers about and awakened all who had been sleeping.

A gun battle ensued, and Ledbetter and the other lawmen were able to keep the robbers from reaching the express car. Texas Jack did, however, manage to board a passenger car and rob its occupants. He made his way through all the passengers, but upon reaching the express car, he was promptly shot by Ledbetter.

One of his gang members helped him get away, but he nearly died from the wound. It was while he was recovering at his brother's home in Arkansas that Texas Jack repented of his outlaw ways. He surrendered to federal marshals and was sentenced by Judge Isaac Parker. After serving a short prison term, Reed joined a Wild West show and went on the lecture circuit, declaring to his audiences that crime doesn't pay.

CHAPTER 7

THE CHIEFS

OSAGE CHIEF OVERSAW NATION'S WEALTH

His birth name was Wah-She-Hah, which means Star That Travels. In later years, this Osage statesman was known as Chief Bacon Rind. Born on the Osage Reservation in what is today Kansas, Bacon Rind came to Indian Territory with his people when they returned in 1871.

Unlike most of the tribes that were removed to the territory, the Osages actually bought the land that would eventually become Osage County, Oklahoma. Their title deed made all the difference in their successes and their struggles on an oil-rich land. Progressive leaders like Bacon Rind had made sure that their deed included the mineral rights.

Bacon Rind was considered a traditionalist, for he retained many of the customs and dress of the Osages even as he traveled frequently to Washington to speak on behalf of his people. But he favored allotment of the land to individual tribal members and oversaw the development of their oil and natural gas resources. Under his leadership in the early twentieth century, the Osages transitioned from a life of subsistence to being the richest people on earth.

Bacon Rind first served as a tribal councilor and then assistant chief from 1904 to 1905. He was elected principal chief in 1912. This was a pivotal time for the Osages. Oil was just starting to be commercially extracted and refined in Oklahoma. Oil men were rushing to the young state to bid for the opportunity to develop the massive oil reserves under the soil.

Chief Bacon Rind oversaw the process of selling oil leases to the wildcatters who flooded the Osage Nation. He worked with an auctioneer named Colonel Walters who had been born in Illinois but at a young age had moved with his family to Indian Territory and grew up near Chouteau. Walters became a good friend to Bacon Rind after he was hired as the official auctioneer for the Osages, and he worked to get the best price for each oil lease he auctioned. While in their employ, Walters settled in the little town of Skedee.

In a single day, Walters auctioned $1 million worth of leases under an elm tree in Pawhuska. That tree became known as the Million Dollar Elm. In total, Bacon Rind and Walters saw over $150 million in oil leases sold in about a fifteen-year period.

Walters was so pleased with his work and his friendship with the Osage chief that he commissioned a statue of the two men shaking hands. The statue was erected at the main intersection in Skedee and was titled *Bond of Friendship*.

Bacon Rind, like nearly every Osage on the reservation, became a millionaire. He built a fine home in Pawhuska but kept many of the traditions of his people. For the last decades of his life, he traveled nearly every year to Washington to protect the interests of his tribe. He died in Pawhuska in 1932 and was buried in a nearby cemetery.

"LONG JOHN" WAS LOYAL SEMINOLE LEADER

John Chupco was a full-blood Seminole born in the Florida Everglades around 1821. In his early thirties, the tall and athletic Chupco had become a chief of the "Newcomer Band" of Seminoles and helped to lead them during their forced removal to Indian Territory in 1855.

In 1861, when Albert Pike approached the Five Tribes seeking alliance treaties with the Confederacy, Chupco was an outspoken opponent of the Seminole treaty and refused to sign it as a town chief. Gathering other like-minded members of his nation, Chupco, along with another town leader named Billy Bowlegs, joined forces with Opothle Yahola, the Creek leader of those Indians who wished to remain loyal to their treaties with the United States.

This group was camping together in the Creek Nation when they were attacked by Confederate forces in December 1861. Forced to flee, Yahola and Chupco led the Loyals toward Kansas, fighting three skirmishes along the way. They eventually found refuge near Fort Scott but were destitute and demoralized by the time they arrived. They would spend a miserable winter of 1862 in Kansas.

Chupco, along with a number of Creek and Seminole men, enlisted in the Union army and formed the First Indian Home Guard. Chupco was a sergeant in Company F of the First Regiment. He would also become the chief of the Loyal Seminoles and served these Northern sympathizers throughout the Civil War years. Because of his height—six foot seven inches—Chupco gained the nickname "Long John" from his fellow soldiers.

After the war, Chupco continued as chief of the Loyal Seminoles while John Jumper was chief of the Confederate sympathizers. "Long John" represented his people at the negotiations for the Reconstruction Treaty of 1866 held in Fort Smith. From the signing of the treaty, Chupco was recognized by the federal government as the Seminole chief until his death.

The Seminoles, like the other tribes, faced the enormous task of rebuilding their nation that had been destroyed by the war. Chupco expected every Seminole to help in this building process and would levy fines against anyone caught loafing. He reestablished his own farm and ranch with about 140 acres in crop production and a large herd of livestock. In 1869, he joined the Presbyterian congregation in the Seminole capital of Wewoka.

One story is told that demonstrates Long John's enormous stride and stamina. It is said that he walked from Little River to Fort Gibson in a single day—a distance of about one hundred miles. How many hours this "day" included is unclear, but he had to have walked over five miles per hour to have completed this journey.

The Reconstruction treaties signed by the Five Tribes in 1866 required them to form a true territory. In compliance with this stipulation, the tribes met in Okmulgee in 1870 to write a constitution and form a government. Chupco and many other members of the tribes were opposed to ending their national sovereignty, so ultimately, the constitution was rejected by a vote of tribal citizens.

Chupco continued his service as Seminole chief until his death in 1881 at age sixty. Though he had never received much formal education, he had been viewed as an able administrator who served his people well.

APACHE WARRIOR SPENT FINAL YEARS IN OKLAHOMA

From the time of Spanish settlement in the Southwest, clashes with the Apaches were ongoing. Following the Mexican-American War, when the United States acquired the ancestral lands of the Apaches, the warriors and chiefs of that tribe extended their conflict to include American troops.

The most famous of the Apache fighters was a warrior named Goyahkla, whom Mexican troops called Geronimo. After these troops killed several members of his family in 1850, Geronimo vowed to take revenge and entered into a long-running feud that lasted for years. Fighting alongside other Apaches such as Cochise, Geronimo gained a reputation for being a crafty military leader who continually eluded capture. Newspaper accounts of his exploits made him one of the most famous American Indians during the 1870s and 1880s.

Continually hunted by Mexican and American troops, Geronimo tried more than once to strike a peace deal and settle with his people on a reservation in Arizona. But such confinement was untenable for a people used to a nomadic life, and after a time, Geronimo and his followers would strike out on raids that would bring military pursuit again.

In 1885, Geronimo left the Arizona reservation with a small band of followers. General George Crook, with two cavalry units that included Apache scouts, pursued the warrior into Mexico. Geronimo managed to elude capture for nearly a year, but eventually, exhaustion forced him to surrender once again. He suggested a meeting place at Fort Bowie in Arizona to discuss terms of peace with the army.

But hearing rumors that he and his men would be massacred when they reached the United States, Geronimo slipped away once again. General Crook was dismissed and replaced by General Nelson Miles. The new commander sent Captain Henry Lawton with the Fourth Cavalry in pursuit, and Lawton was able to bring Geronimo back to the reservation.

General Miles quickly sent Geronimo to Florida as a prisoner of war to avoid any further conflict in Arizona. In time, other Apaches joined Geronimo there, and thousands of tourists came to see the famous Indian warrior. After a time, Geronimo was transferred to Fort Sill, Oklahoma Territory, in 1894. Traveling by train, he was greeted at every stop by curious crowds seeking a photo, autograph or some other souvenir. Geronimo sold the buttons off his coat and his hat while stopped at one depot. At the next town, he bought more buttons and hats. He had just enough time to sew the new buttons on his coat before arriving at the next stop. Here he would sell

Apache warrior Geronimo. *Oklahoma Historical Society.*

the buttons and his hat once again. He had collected a nice sum of money by the time he reached his final home at Fort Sill.

Geronimo and other Apache "prisoners of war" were given individual land allotments at Fort Sill. Here the old warrior joined the church, became a farmer and settled into a life of peace. He was allowed to travel, however, and he continued to take advantage of his celebrity status. He was paid for his appearance at the 1904 St. Louis World's Fair and to ride in President

Theodore Roosevelt's inaugural parade in Washington in 1905. He traveled for a time with Pawnee Bill's Wild West Show.

The last great warrior lived out his remaining years at Fort Sill. Geronimo died in 1909 and was buried in the Fort Sill Apache Cemetery.

FATE OF CRAZY SNAKE REMAINS A MYSTERY

The decision of the federal government to allot the lands of the Five Civilized Tribes was initially opposed by those tribes. It took years of negotiations to craft allotment treaties that provided for the enrollment of tribal members and the allotment of tribal lands.

Despite the treaties, though, some members of the tribes were adamantly, even violently opposed to accepting allotments. In the Creek Nation, the most vigorous opposition came from a full-blood Indian named Chitto Harjo. His English name was Wilson Jones, but he became known as Crazy Snake. Chitto is from the Creek word meaning "snake," and Harjo, a common surname among Creeks, means "recklessly brave" or "crazy."

Chitto Harjo was born in 1846 in Arbeka town in Indian Territory. The Arbekas were considered to be gatekeepers for the tribe who gave warning of coming danger. Crazy Snake sounded a warning about allotments, taking his efforts to derail the process all the way to Washington, where he met with President Theodore Roosevelt.

Crazy Snake soon had a following of other tribal members—primarily full-bloods and freedmen. They gathered at a place known as the Hickory Stomp Grounds in McIntosh County. Here Harjo formed his own tribal government in October 1900, with himself as chief.

Harjo attempted to enforce old tribal laws upon Creeks living in the area. They complained to federal authorities in Muskogee, and a long-running conflict developed between the "Snakes," as Harjo's followers were called, and law enforcement authorities. Crazy Snake himself was arrested more than once and brought to the federal jail in Muskogee.

Even after statehood, the Crazy Snake Rebellion lingered. The Snakes continued to congregate at the stomp grounds, creating fear and distrust among people who lived in the area. In March 1909, a large-scale theft of salt pork from smokehouses around the community of Pierce occurred. Complaints reached McIntosh Country sheriff William Odom accusing the Snakes of the thefts.

The log cabin of Crazy Snake was later set on fire by his followers. *Oklahoma Historical Society*.

Over the next five days, several posses were sent to the stomp grounds, each time meeting armed resistance. It is believed that Crazy Snake was wounded in one of the gun battles. Sheriff Odom's own son, Herman Odom, and another deputy named Ed Baum were killed in a fight at Crazy Snake's home near Pierce. Harjo's home was set on fire by the Snakes themselves before they fled into the surrounding hills.

Sheriff Odom telephoned Governor Charles Haskell in Guthrie and requested the state militia be called out. Haskell complied and sent troops out from Muskogee. They combed the area around the stomp grounds, making arrests of several Snakes.

Their leader was never found, however, and his whereabouts became a question that has never been satisfactorily answered. Some believe Harjo escaped the gun battle, crossed the Canadian River and died at the home of a Choctaw friend. Others conjectured that his wounds were not serious and he made it all the way to Mexico and lived out his life there. Still others theorize that he died in his home and the Snakes set it on fire to keep his body from falling into the hands of authorities. The real answer will probably never be known.

CHIEF PERRYMAN PUT OKLAHOMA UP FOR SALE

Legust Chouteau Perryman was born near Tullahassee Mission in 1837. He was from a prominent Creek family, his parents, Lewis and Ellen Perryman, having moved from Alabama to Indian Territory in 1828. Perryman's uncle George owned a large cattle ranch in the area that became Tulsa.

L.C. Perryman was educated at the Tullahassee Mission School and proved to be a fine scholar. His skills in mathematics and languages would serve him well in his future political career. He devoted much time to translating hymns and scripture into Creek and later in life translated Creek law from English into the Muscogee language.

During the Civil War, Perryman served in the Union army as a private in the First Regiment of the Indian Home Guard. As such, he stood across the battle line from a fellow student of the mission schools and another future Creek chief: Pleasant Porter.

Following the war, Perryman was involved in the reconstruction of the Creek Nation and worked on the formation of a new constitution and government. He served for six years as a judge in the Coweta District of the nation. He then was elected in 1874 to represent his town of Big Spring in the legislative House of Warriors.

While serving in the Creek legislature, he was sent to Washington on several occasions as a national delegate. In Washington, Perryman introduced a controversial proposal: to sell the Oklahoma lands the Creeks had ceded in their 1866 Reconstruction treaty. At that time, the Creeks had agreed to cede the lands for thirty cents an acre. Over the years, other Plains tribes were moved onto these lands, but a large tract remained unassigned.

Perryman proposed that the government pay the Creeks $1.25 per acre and then open these remaining lands for non-Indian settlement. His political opponents were furious at the proposal, and for a number of years, nothing came of it.

When Perryman ran for chief in 1887, his opposition used his proposal in campaigning against him. But Perryman won the election, and shortly after being sworn in as chief, he took up the negotiations with the U.S. government for the Oklahoma sale. It brought much-needed cash into the Creek coffers and led to the Oklahoma land run of 1889.

CHAPTER 8

SOME "SHEROES"

TITANIC SURVIVOR WROTE OKLAHOMA ROMANCE

Helen Candee wrote about the fateful voyage aboard the *Titanic* cruise liner. She tells of a shipboard romance in which she and a younger man sneaked onto the crewmen's deck to stand at the bow and watch the majestic boat pierce the waves. It was not a work of fiction. The well-known author knew this *Titanic* experience firsthand.

Helen was born in Brooklyn, New York, in 1858 to Henry and Mary (Churchill) Hungerford and was a *Mayflower* descendant. Her father and maternal grandfather were successful merchants. While she was still young, the family moved to Connecticut, where she received her education. From her mother, Helen learned the art of being a fine hostess and making a name for herself in the upper-class social scene.

In 1880, Helen married a prominent businessman named Edward Candee. They had two children, Edith and Harold, but their fifteen years of marriage were unhappy. Edward was an abusive alcoholic, and in 1895, her well-connected parents secured a legal separation for Helen. She could not, however, secure a divorce in Connecticut. For this reason, Candee took her two young children and headed west. It was known that the divorce laws in the new Oklahoma Territory were more lenient, and Helen was not the only person to take up residence in the territory in order to end a marriage. A divorce decree could be obtained after a mandatory ninety-day residency.

Guthrie pharmacist F.B. Lillie and his wife offered Candee and her children a place to stay. She enjoyed the adventure of living in the West and stayed in Oklahoma Territory longer than the ninety days required. She hired attorney Henry Asp to assist her in her divorce proceedings.

While living in the territory, she wrote articles on the land runs and the issue of statehood for eager readers back east. Her journalism, painting an attractive picture of the Twin Territories, encouraged more settlement and some believe helped to push the statehood issue forward.

Candee wrote a seminal book, a first in feminist circles, titled *How Women May Earn a Living*. In 1901, she published one of her few works of fiction, a novel titled *An Oklahoma Romance*. Set in Guthrie, it dealt with a land claim dispute following the 1889 land run. It was lauded by critics and widely read by her fans.

Eventually, Candee left Oklahoma and settled in Washington, D.C., where she again entered the social scene. She gained a reputation as an interior designer, specializing in working with antiques. She worked with architect Nathan Wyeth on several projects, including an expansion of the West Wing of the White House.

Candee wrote several books on women's issues and interior design. The income allowed her to build a summer home in Maine, and her time was spent between her two residences and visits to her married daughter in New York. Her son, Harold, kept a stable of fine horses in Virginia, and Candee loved to ride. She was one of the first women in the East to ride astride, a skill she likely gained while living in Oklahoma.

In 1912, Helen traveled to Europe doing research for a new decorating book. While there, she received word that Harold had been seriously injured in a fall from a horse. She immediately booked passage home aboard a new luxury liner, the *Titanic*.

When the disaster began to play out after an iceberg struck the ship, a London investor named Hugh Woolner assisted Helen into Lifeboat Number 6. Candee broke her ankle when she jumped into the small craft but survived the fall. She assisted the "unsinkable" Molly Brown in rowing the lifeboat to the rescue vessel, the *Carpathia*.

Upon reaching New York, Candee was taken to a hospital for a few days, and then after she was released, she hurried to visit her son in a nearby hospital. Both of them recovered from their injuries. The harrowing experience made Candee a celebrity along with all the other survivors.

Though Candee had to walk with a cane for the remainder of her years, that didn't keep her out of the saddle. She rode with fellow suffragists in the inaugural parade in Washington for President Woodrow Wilson. She considered her march with ten thousand women for the vote one of her greatest moments.

Candee continued an active life of writing, decorating and entertaining. She engaged in Red Cross work during the world wars. She spent the last months of her life at her retreat in Maine and died at age ninety on August 23, 1949.

WEBBERS FALLS EXISTS BECAUSE OF A WOMAN'S COURAGE

Many towns in Oklahoma have nearly faced extinction at some time in their history due to fire, flood or tornado. Some towns never recover from a disaster and become little more than ghost towns at the end of dirt roads, just a shadowed reminder of their former selves. Other towns are inspired to fight back after devastating loss to rebuild and keep their town alive.

The town of Webbers Falls had to rebuild more than once in its long history. This community, named for Cherokee leader Walter Webber, was established early in the state's history, gaining a post office in 1856. Its residents witnessed the conflict of the Civil War as few towns in Indian Territory did. Union forces practically wiped out the town with fire in 1863.

But its Cherokee citizens returned after the war and rebuilt the river town where steamboats frequently stopped to wait for higher water levels to make it over the falls on the Arkansas River. The little town prospered and developed a thriving downtown of mercantiles and cotton gins.

Then on March 11, 1911, fire once again threatened the town. A clerk at the Hayes Mercantile stepped into the back warehouse for an item and glanced out the window. A blaze whipped by strong winds was already engulfing much of the downtown district. There was little time to take action to fight the fire.

In one of the downtown buildings, a nineteen-year-old telephone operator named Rose Coppinger was working at the town's central switchboard. In those days, all calls were still handled through a local switchboard, and the operator generally knew everyone in town.

Young Rose stayed at her switchboard despite the smoke, heat and flames and calmly but quickly notified residents about the fire. One by one, she connected to telephones throughout the town to let people know

This telephone exchange would have been similar to the one used by Coppinger.

of the danger, though others urged her to flee the flames. She had to be carried from the burning building wrapped in a wet blanket to make it through the inferno.

Despite Rose's efforts though, much of the downtown was destroyed. Most residences were spared when firefighters made a stand at the Hayes Mercantile and finally got the flames under control there. Several stores, two banks, restaurants, drugstores, cotton gins and pool halls were all gone in a matter of hours.

The citizens of Webbers Falls were inspired by the courage of Rose Coppinger. They petitioned and won for her a Carnegie Medal for Heroism and took up a collection totaling $500 as a token of their esteem. Since Rose had lost what belongings she had in the burned building, this act of gratitude was very helpful to her.

Businessmen in Webbers Falls met at the Hayes Mercantile the evening after the fire. With Rose's courage fresh in their minds, they each one vowed to rebuild their businesses. Tents were set up in town until new buildings could be erected. Surveyors came the following week and laid out new streets. Webbers Falls, inspired by a young woman's courage, turned this tragedy into a triumph over adversity to build back the town better than before.

"CREEK POCAHONTAS" SETTLED AT THE THREE FORKS

In 1818, the Seminole War was being fought in Spanish Florida. General Andrew Jackson had moved troops, including the Georgia militia, into Florida in a military campaign meant to contain the more violent members of the Creek and Seminole tribes, as well as runaway slaves who effectively hid out in the Florida wilderness. The fighting was centered near a Creek village called Francis Town, named for Chief Hillis Hadjo, who was known to Americans as Francis the Prophet.

The Georgia militia had bivouacked at Fort Gadsden near Francis Town. A young private named Duncan McKrimmon went out fishing on the Apalachicola River and lost his way. He was captured by a band of Creeks and was taken to Francis Town. They intended to kill the young man to avenge the deaths of some family members at the hands of the military.

Chief Hillis Hadjo's youngest daughter, fifteen-year-old Milly, was present when Private McKrimmon was brought into the village. The young man was stripped and bound, and his captors danced in victory around him.

The stone monument honors the Creek Pocahontas, Milly Francis. *Author collection.*

Milly appealed to her father to spare the young man's life, but he told her she would have to convince those who were avenging their family.

Just as the execution was about to take place, Milly stepped in, declaring they would have to take her life as well. She argued that McKrimmon was too young to be responsible for what the military did and should not be punished for a crime he had not committed.

The young man's life was spared, and some weeks later, Hadjo sold McKrimmon to the Spanish for seven and a half gallons of rum. The Spanish returned McKrimmon to the Georgia militia, and the story of Milly's brave rescue spread through the ranks. She became known as the "Creek Pocahontas."

As the Seminole War continued, Milly Francis and members of her family and village surrendered at Fort Gadsden in a state of destitution and near-starvation. Colonel Matthew Arbuckle, commander at Fort Gadsden, recognized Milly to be the famed "Pocahontas" and saw to it that she and her family were treated well.

After being detained some time at Fort Gadsden, the Creeks were moved to Indian Territory. There, Milly Francis married and had a home on the south bank of the Arkansas River two or three miles west of the Grand River, somewhere in the vicinity of Bacone College.

At age forty-five, she was widowed, destitute again and in poor health. General Ethan Allen Hitchcock, sent to Indian Territory to investigate the treatment of the Indians, brought her condition to the attention of Congress and attained for her a yearly stipend of ninety-six dollars and an honorary medal.

Unfortunately, Milly died before receiving either the money or the medal. She was buried near her home, but her grave site is unknown today. A monument to Milly Francis, the Creek Pocahontas, stands on the Bacone College campus in Muskogee.

CREEK WOMAN SHOWED COURAGE IN FACE OF OPPOSITION

When the Five Civilized Tribes were removed to Indian Territory in the 1830s, many missionaries made the move with them. Presbyterian, Methodist and Baptist missions had operated schools and churches among the tribes in their homelands in the southeastern United States. The missionaries, most of whom were New Englanders, chose to travel west with the Five Tribes in order to continue their work among the people they had come to respect and love.

As the first Creek immigrants settled along the Arkansas and Verdigris Rivers, new missions, schools and churches were organized in the new Creek Nation. One of the earliest churches was the Muscogee Baptist Church located just north of the Arkansas River. Presbyterian missions later were located at Koweta and Tullahassee. The Methodists operated Asbury Mission near North Fork Town.

In 1836, a second group of Creeks arrived in Indian Territory. These were the Upper Creeks who were opposed to the work of the missionaries. They felt these New Englanders were preaching against slavery and were pulling Creeks away from their old traditions and beliefs, so they persuaded the Creek Council to outlaw missionary work in the Creek Nation.

Chief Roley McIntosh asked the Indian superintendent to order all missionaries to leave. Many of the missionaries and members of their congregations simply moved into the Cherokee and Choctaw Nations and continued to meet for Sunday services. The Creek law even went so far as to make praying a crime punishable with lashes on the back. Still, many Creeks quietly refused to give up their faith even in the face of such a strict punishment.

It is unclear how many Creeks faced the switch, but the last known survivor of a whipping was a Creek woman named Sallie Logan. According to stories handed down about her, Sallie fainted at the whipping tree but revived some time later. She painfully crawled to a nearby spring and washed her bleeding back. Then she walked ten miles to church.

No Creek ever recanted their faith. Within a few years, the law was repealed and worship was allowed again. In fact, Roley McIntosh became a Baptist minister, and a future Creek chief, Samuel Checote, became a Methodist preacher who helped build many of the early Methodist churches in the Creek Nation.

CHAPTER 9

THE CATTLEMEN

POWER COUPLE FOUND SUCCESS IN POTAWATOMI NATION

William Greiffenstein was born in Germany in 1829, immigrated to America in 1848 and settled in Kansas. Trained in the mercantile business, Greiffenstein traded with different Indian tribes of the Plains both in Kansas and Indian Territory. He married a full-blood Cheyenne named Jennie, and her connections opened doors for trade with the Cheyenne, Apache, Arapaho, Comanche and Kiowa nations.

By 1867, Greiffenstein had trading posts on both the Canadian and Washita Rivers in western Indian Territory. Known as "Dutch Bill" by friends and fellow traders such as Jesse Chisholm and James Mead, the merchant was skilled in dealing with the Indians who came to trade with him. But General Philip Sheridan accused Greiffenstein of selling firearms to tribal members and had him thrown out of the territory. He appealed his case to Washington and was compensated for the loss of the goods he left behind.

Greiffenstein then settled on the Arkansas River in central Kansas and helped to establish the town of Wichita. After his first wife died, William married Catherine Burnett, a daughter of the Potawatomi chief Abram Burnett. Catherine's mother was also a native of Germany. William and Catherine operated a store in Wichita and made a fortune in real estate. He even served as mayor of that city from 1880 to 1884.

Founder of Wichita William
Greiffenstein. *National Park Service*.

The Potawatomi people were moved into Indian Territory, giving Catherine access to land there. In 1883, the couple claimed four thousand acres of land in the Potawatomi Nation. They developed a ranch in Catherine's name and ran large herds of cattle, horses and hogs.

When allotments were being made in 1888, the Interior Department ordered the Greiffensteins to shut down their ranch and move the animals to Catherine's 160-acre allotment. Unable to support such large herds on this acreage, the couple was forced to sell most of the animals. But until the land run of 1891, the Greiffensteins continued to graze their remaining herds on nearby unclaimed land.

Besides their ranch, the Greiffensteins also opened a store on Catherine's allotment. William planned to develop a town around the store after Oklahoma Territory was created, and he called it Burnett for Catherine and her family. They built a fine ranch house near the store and in 1895 moved permanently to Burnett, where they lived out the remainder of their lives.

WEALTHY CATTLEMAN OPPOSED ALLOTMENT

Wilson Nathaniel Jones was born in the old Choctaw Nation of Mississippi around 1827. He came with his family to Indian Territory in 1833 in the first removal of the Choctaws following the Treaty of Dancing Rabbit Creek. They settled along the Little River in a beautiful rural area where access to education was limited. Nevertheless, he was self-taught and gave himself a foundation for later success in life.

Following the Civil War, Jones built a home on Shawnee Creek near the small settlement of Cade. Here he farmed and ran a little general store. He married, though his wife's name is unknown, and had eight children.

At age forty, in 1867, he formed a partnership with James Myers, and they went into the ranching business. Jones showed a great acumen for this occupation, and within a few years, the partners owned a herd of over one thousand head of cattle. Unfortunately, Myers proved to be untrustworthy. With the demand for beef high, prices were also high, and money could be made selling to the northern markets. Myers sold the herd in 1871, likely to a Texas ranch crew driving cattle to market on the nearby Shawnee Cattle Trail. Myers then fled the area with the profits, leaving Jones with nothing but debts.

Wilson Jones slowly worked his way back to a position of wealth, and by 1890, his ranch contained seventeen thousand acres of land. He was reportedly one of the richest men in the Choctaw Nation. He put over five hundred acres into crop production and grazed cattle on the remaining land. His brand, the WJ, marked over five thousand beeves.

Besides ranching, Jones also invested in cotton and coal and opened another store in nearby Caddo. His obvious skill with handling money led to his election as Choctaw national treasurer in 1887. He ran for principal chief the following year but was defeated. He tried again in 1890 and defeated the incumbent chief, Benjamin Smallwood.

As chief, Jones pushed for continued support of education in the Choctaw Nation. A boys' boarding school was established in 1892 near Hartshorne and was named Jones Academy in his honor.

After serving two terms, Jones retired from politics for a time but ran again in 1898 when allotments were the primary topic of debate during the election. Jones was opposed to allotments, as were all the ranchers among the Five Tribes. None were willing to give up the fine acreages they had spent years developing to be "given" a 160-acre allotment. However, he was defeated by the pro-allotment incumbent, Green McCurtain.

Jones did not live to see his ranch broken up. He died in 1901 at age seventy-four, leaving a large estate to his family. He was buried in the family cemetery on his ranch near Cade. The road running nearby today is called Wilson N. Jones Road.

MILLER RANCH HAD BEGINNINGS IN GREEN COUNTRY

Following the Civil War, Colonel George Miller brought his wife and infant son west from Kentucky. It was his intent to travel as far west as the railroad would take them and then continue on by covered wagon to California.

The Miller family arrived in Springfield, Missouri, which at the time was the end of the line for the railroad. They secured a wagon and made it to Newtonia, Missouri, right on the state line across from Indian Territory. Miller was so impressed with the rich prairie of the territory that he decided to stay in the area and try his hand at ranching.

The Millers settled in Baxter Springs and added to their family while George learned the cowboy trade. His oldest son, Joseph, followed him everywhere and learned alongside his father. Together they began to herd cattle from Texas along the East Shawnee Cattle Trail up to the railheads of Kansas, all the while building their own herd that grazed on Indian-owned land they leased south of Baxter Springs.

The Miller Ranch adopted a brand of 101. After the opening of the Cherokee Strip through a land run in 1893, the family moved to a location near the land assigned to the Ponca tribe. The ranch became known as the 101 Ranch at that time.

The Millers enjoyed good relations with the Poncas, and George and Joseph were made honorary tribal members. George died in 1902, but his three sons—Joseph, Zach and George Jr.—continued to grow the ranch until it contained over 100,000 acres of land.

Joseph, or Colonel Joe, as he was called, ran the ranch and also was in charge of the Wild West show that developed there. He made the ranch a showplace that drew visitors from around the world. He also traveled the world with his western production that included many of his Ponca friends.

Well-liked and respected by employees, the Poncas and the townsfolk of Ponca City, Colonel Joe was known as a tough but fair man. One incident is told about two roustabouts who worked on the Wild West show. They fell

Ranch owner George Miller Jr. *Oklahoma Historical Society.*

into an argument, each accusing the other of cheating (probably at cards). Joe was told of the fight and had both men brought to him. He ordered them to empty their pockets of all their money. Then he divided it evenly between them and sent them on their way—one heading south of the ranch and one going north.

Joe helped to organize the Cherokee Strip Cow Punchers Association and was voted in as "president for life." The group of old cowmen held their annual meeting at the 101 Ranch until Joe's death in 1927 at the young age of fifty-eight. He had died as he always said he wanted to— while still in the harness. Over five thousand people attended his funeral at the ranch he had helped his father found first in the green fields of northeast Oklahoma.

PICKETT PIONEERED RODEO FAVORITE

Like many young men in Texas following the Civil War, the career of Bill Pickett began with work on a ranch. Born in Williamson County, Texas, in 1870, Pickett was a descendant of slaves and also had Cherokee heritage. One of thirteen children, Pickett completed the fifth grade, which was the standard for education in that day, and was likely working in the cattle industry by his early teens.

He honed the skills of riding and roping necessary for any cowboy as he worked on ranches in the area of Taylor, Texas. Roundups and brandings in the spring and fall gave the cowboys all the work they could handle. They learned to rely on the smart cow dogs that kept the cattle in line. Pickett observed the technique employed by the dogs of nipping the nose or lip of a steer or cow to keep it moving or bring it under control. He tried this technique himself while wrestling yearlings for the branding iron. Surprisingly, it worked, and he became quite skilled at "bulldogging," as it came to be called. The other cowboys surely got a kick out of watching him rope a steer then grab it by the horns, bite it on the lip and fall backward, bringing the animal down easily.

Pickett soon realized people would pay money to watch his unique cowboy skill. He started performing at county fairs and rodeos and afterward passing the hat for donations. His reputation grew, and with four of his brothers, he started a business called Pickett Brothers Bronco Busters and Rough Riders Association in Taylor. It was also here that Bill served in the National Guard and as deacon in his church and married his sweetheart, Maggie Turner.

Cowboys had always competed with one another on the ranches, showing off their roping and riding skills. These impromptu competitions eventually grew into professional rodeos held all over the American West. Pickett began to compete in Texas and Wyoming and Arizona and Oklahoma Territories. Other cowhands copied his steer wrestling technique, and that sport became an important part of every rodeo.

By 1904, Pickett had a well-established reputation as a great performer at rodeos, including the prestigious Cheyenne Frontier Days. If blacks were not allowed to compete in a rodeo, he claimed his Indian heritage and was not challenged. Rodeo organizers were likely eager to have the popular cowboy in their lineup.

He caught the eye of the Miller brothers, who owned the 101 Ranch near Ponca City in Oklahoma Territory. In 1905, they hired Pickett to be a part of their Wild West show. Bill moved his family of nine children to the 101 Ranch, and when not performing at shows across America and Europe, he worked as a ranch hand.

The Wild West shows of the early 1900s naturally translated into other entertainment, including vaudeville and the movies. Pickett starred in several films, most notably the Richard Norman productions of *The Bull-Dogger* and *The Crimson Skull*, which were filmed in Oklahoma.

Pickett was still working at the 101 in the 1930s but died in 1932 after being kicked by a horse. He was buried near the White Eagle Monument north of Marland, Oklahoma. In 1989, he was inducted into the Rodeo Hall of Fame of the Western Heritage Museum in Oklahoma City.

SEVERS STRETCHED HIS EMPIRE ACROSS CREEK NATION

Frederick B. Severs was one of those rugged frontier pioneers who made such a difference in his community that his name lived on well after his death. He had a hand in much of the early history of both Okmulgee and Muskogee.

Severs was born in Arkansas in 1835 near the border with the Cherokee Nation. He attended Cane Hill Collegiate Institute in Arkansas, and after graduating at age seventeen, he moved to Indian Territory. An old friend of his father's gave him a job in a mercantile in Fort Gibson.

At age twenty, Severs was asked by the Creek Nation to lead a school at Concharty, near present-day Haskell. Here he met another schoolteacher named Annie Anderson, who later became his wife. Annie was the daughter of George Anderson, a Creek chief.

Leaving the school in 1860, Severs next returned to the mercantile trade, starting a store in Shieldsville, a small community near Okmulgee. Before he could make a success of this business, however, the Civil War broke out and disrupted life in Indian Territory.

Severs joined a Confederate regiment organized by Samuel Checote and was given the rank of second lieutenant. He was one of very few soldiers in the regiment who was not Creek. By the end of the war, he held the rank of captain and was referred to as Captain Severs for the remainder of his life.

Starting over after the war was difficult for everyone, but Severs returned to his store in Shieldsville and slowly built the business. Eventually, he moved it to the Creek capital, Okmulgee, where he also had a cotton gin and sawmill. During this time, he was also made an adopted member of the Creek tribe and became very involved in Creek national politics.

In 1884, Severs moved to the growing community of Muskogee, buying a business located at Main and Okmulgee Avenue. Quickly, he became one of the leading businessmen in his new hometown. He built a large home at Fifth and Broadway in the center of a four-block area that now includes both the county and federal courthouses.

This J.F. Standiford photo shows the Severs Block in Muskogee under construction. *Author collection.*

Severs was a charter founder of the first bank in Indian Territory and built a large brick structure to house the bank. Known as the Severs Block today, this commercial section between Broadway and Okmulgee at Main is now in the National Register of Historic Places. In Okmulgee, he also helped to establish a bank and built a structure that is also called the Severs Block.

As a Creek citizen, Severs could claim land in the nation, and he developed a large ranch between Okmulgee and Muskogee. His ranch home located about halfway between the two towns was called Pecan Grove. He ran thousands of head of cattle and hogs on his ranch.

Severs's best-known contribution to Muskogee's downtown is the Severs Hotel, which was completed in 1912. Severs moved his home to the Capitol Place area in order to make room for the hotel. Now Muskogee's tallest downtown structure, the Severs Building stands as a testimony of the long influence of a successful and generous businessman.

CHAPTER 10

THE MEDICAL PIONEERS

SINGING DENTIST OFFERED MINISTRY
AND SERVICE TO INDIAN TERRITORY

When Indian Territory's first dentist, Dr. Albert Bonnell, arrived in Muskogee in 1888, he quickly became involved in the community he would serve. Because Dr. Bonnell's office in Muskogee was the first dental practice in the entire Indian Territory, there was a great demand for his services. He proved popular also for his love of music and had a great talent for singing.

Also arriving in Muskogee the same year was Bessie Weir, who had come to teach music at Harrell International Institute. Harrell Institute had been established in 1879 as an elementary school by the Methodist congregation that met in the Rock Church at Cherokee Street and Okmulgee Avenue. The school was later expanded to include high school. Many students who lived too far away to walk to school each day boarded at the Rock Church parsonage.

Dr. Bonnell joined the Rock Church and began singing in the choir. It is probably here that he met Bessie Weir. They were married in 1896 and later had a son named Albert Jr. The Bonnells were passionate about music and promoted musical events in Muskogee at every opportunity. Dr. Bonnell also played in Maddin's Mechanical Band, a private group made up mostly of employees at the Maddin Hardware Store.

The singing dentist must have been quite talented, for in addition to singing in the church choir for over fifty years, he also was frequently asked to solo at funerals. It's estimated that he sang at more than two thousand funerals over his lifetime. He was so dedicated to this ministry to the bereaved that he would not hesitate to close his dental office when it was necessary.

Young Albert Bonnell Jr. followed in his father's footsteps in many ways. He, too, chose the practice of dentistry for his career and took over his father's office in Muskogee. Between them, they had over ninety years of dental practice in the city. Like his father, Albert Jr. served as president of the State Dental Association, the first son of a former president to hold this position. The elder Dr. Bonnell also served as vice president of the American Dental Association and was appointed by Governor Charles Haskell to the State Dental Board.

Albert Jr. followed his father's service on the Muskogee School Board. Albert Sr. served ten years on the school board, while Albert Jr. served fifteen. They also both served on the Muskogee City Council for a number of years.

CALLAHANS WERE A PROMINENT CREEK FAMILY

The Callahan family was prominent in Muskogee and the Creek Nation for many years. Samuel B. Callahan was a mixed-blood Creek who had been educated in Texas but had settled in the Creek Nation near Okmulgee at the age of twenty-five in 1858.

At the outbreak of the Civil War, Sam Callahan joined the First Creek Mounted Volunteers and attained the rank of captain. In 1864, he was elected to represent the Creek and Seminole Nations in the Confederate Congress in Virginia.

After the war, Captain Callahan returned to Sulphur Springs, Texas, where the family had apparently spent the war years. They again settled in the Creek Nation, this time near what would be Muskogee. Callahan worked as a rancher and farmer and raised a large family. He was active in Creek Nation political affairs and served in the House of Kings.

His son James Oliver Callahan attended medical school in Missouri but returned to Muskogee to set up practice. He built his home and clinic east of the Katy tracks. Dr. Callahan was a well-respected physician and was instrumental in developing the laws of the Creek Nation regulating the practice of medicine.

Dr. Callahan was a booster of development on the east side of Muskogee, and it was for these efforts that the street where his home was located was named for him. Callahan is credited with helping to secure the location for Central High School and the Carnegie Library.

Dr. Callahan was not the only member of his family known for his accomplishments, however. His sister Alice Callahan is credited by Carolyn Foreman as being the first novelist from Indian Territory. Her novel was published in 1891 and was titled *Wynema: Child of the Forest*.

Another sister, Josephine, married Homer Spaulding, a prominent merchant in Muskogee. The Spauldings were strong supporters of the Methodist Rock Church and rebuilt Harrell Institute after it was destroyed by fire. Spaulding Institute, Spaulding Park and Spaulding Boulevard are named for them—all located on the east side of town.

Dr. Callahan knew tragedy in his life. Shortly after the death of his only son, his wife also passed away. Callahan closed his medical office and left Muskogee, traveling extensively for a year, trying to cope with his grief. He later returned to his Muskogee practice and continued to serve his patients as a compassionate and understanding physician.

EARLY DOCTOR SAW NEED FOR RURAL MEDICINE

After the Civil War, Indian Territory saw a new migration of members of the Five Civilized Tribes from their homes in the southeastern United States. The South was suffering from the effects of the war, and many people sought new opportunities farther west. Many members of the tribes who had come to Indian Territory earlier encouraged this new migration.

In 1870, the Cherokee family of Joseph and Evaline Cobb considered a move west. Relatives who had earlier settled in the territory had written enthusiastic reports about the land to be had in the Cherokee Nation. Cobb sold his farm in Tennessee and moved his family of six children to Indian Territory.

The Cobbs traveled by train to Fort Scott, Kansas. There, family met them and brought them to Tahlequah by wagon. From there, the Cobbs located a farm for sale ten miles north of Fort Gibson and settled in a little log cabin on the prairie in the Cooweescoowee District of the Cherokee Nation about six miles southeast of present Wagoner.

The eldest child of the Cobb family, Isabel, was born in 1858 on the farm near Morgantown. She recalled in later years how shortly after settling in their new home, her mother gave birth to her youngest sister, Addie. It was a difficult delivery, and the family urgently sent for a local midwife to attend her. Her mother survived the delivery, but the lack of a doctor nearby made an impression on young Isabel. It was one she would not forget.

Because there were no schools in the countryside, Isabel was sent to school at the Cherokee Female Seminary in Tahlequah. From Fort Gibson, it was a day's ride in a stagecoach to get back and forth from school. Most girls who attended the seminary boarded at the school and returned home only for holidays or the summer.

Isabel graduated from the Female Seminary in 1879. Wishing to continue her education, she went on to Glendale Female College in Glendale, Ohio. She completed her studies there in 1881.

By this time, Isabel had acquired more education than most young women received in that day. She returned to teach at the Cherokee Female Seminary from 1882 until it burned in 1887.

But she had not forgotten the need for doctors in her home district, so Isabel went on to the Women's Medical College of Pennsylvania in 1888. This school had opened in 1850 and was the first in the world to offer a medical degree to women. Isabel completed her studies there and received a medical degree in 1892.

Following a six-month internship in New York at Staten Island Nursery and Child's Hospital, Cobb returned home in 1893 to practice medicine.

Dr. Cobb made house calls by buggy, often with her ward. *Liz McMahan collection.*

Isabel set up her medical practice not in town but out in the country—working from a farmhouse on the family homestead southeast of Wagoner. Dr. Cobb is believed to be one of the first women to practice medicine west of the Mississippi.

She practiced only within the neighboring areas, rarely seeing more than two hundred patients per year. Known as "Dr. Belle," she primarily cared for women and children. Cobb made house calls to patients in the Wagoner, Fort Gibson and Muskogee area, driving many miles in her horse-drawn buggy.

Dr. Cobb continued in practice in the Three Forks region until her own health declined in the 1930s and she was forced to retire from her practice in the country. A Presbyterian and a Republican, Cobb belonged to a number of Wagoner County literary societies. She never married but adopted a six-year-old Italian orphan in 1895. She died in Wagoner on August 11, 1947.

PIONEER SURGEON BROUGHT BETTER MEDICINE TO TERRITORY

Dr. Francis Bartow Fite arrived in Indian Territory in 1886 after receiving his medical degree at Emory University in Atlanta, Georgia. He joined his older brother in practice in Tahlequah and worked with him there for two years. Then he entered New York Polyclinic Medical School and studied under renowned surgeon Dr. John Wyeth.

At the time of his studies under Dr. Wyeth, the practice of surgery was undergoing dramatic changes. Following the teachings of Dr. Louis Pasteur, surgeons were coming to understand how unseen germs were responsible for infections and how important sanitary and sterile environments were to patient care.

When Dr. Fite returned to Indian Territory in 1889, he settled first in Tahlequah and then moved to Muskogee. That same year, he married Julia Patton of Vinita. They built a fine home at Fourth and Broadway in Muskogee. Dr. Fite's medical office was located on Second Street.

Dr. Fite's skill as a surgeon led him more and more to be called upon to perform emergency operations—often to remove bullets after a gunfight. The doctor once remarked that he had two handfuls of bullets in his office that he had removed from grateful patients. All were neatly tagged with the name of the person they had been removed from.

But Fite was discouraged by the unsanitary conditions he had to work under, often performing surgeries in the homes of his patients. And though he had brought the first X-ray machine to Indian Territory, he found its use limited at his small office.

To improve such medical conditions, Fite established St. Mary's Sanitarium, the first private hospital in Indian Territory. It was located on South Main Street in Muskogee and served patients from as far away as Vinita and McAlester. The name of the sanitarium was later changed to the Martha Robb Hospital.

In 1899, a serious smallpox epidemic swept across the Creek Nation. Dr. Fite's understanding of how germs spread disease made him the best choice to lead the effort

Surgeon Francis B. Fite. *Author collection.*

in fighting the epidemic. The Muskogee City Council, which had been in existence for less than a year, asked Fite and his medical partner, J.L. Blakemore, to take charge of handling the medical crisis.

Using vaccination and strict quarantines, the two doctors were able to stem the spread of the dreaded disease. Dr. Blakemore quarantined the entire town of Okmulgee, and the Muskogee City Council posted armed guards around the perimeter of the city to keep out anyone who had not been vaccinated. Guards also rode the M-K-T rail line and would not let anyone embark upon the trains who had not been vaccinated.

Beyond his medical expertise, Dr. Fite was also very civic minded. He personally undertook the construction of a building suitable for housing the Dawes Commission, thus ensuring it would be headquartered in Muskogee while working on land allotments for Indian Territory. Fite also served two terms as mayor of Muskogee.

CHAPTER II

THE MERCHANTS

EDWARDS'S SETTLEMENT WAS A CROSSROADS

Around 1834, a Creek citizen named James Edwards built a log trading post on the west bank of the Little River where it meets the Canadian. As a southern point of the Creek Nation, it served as an important trading location and a source of protection for both Creeks and Seminoles who were settling in Indian Territory in the late 1820s and early 1830s.

Across the river and north by about a mile stood Fort Holmes, built also to provide protection for the new Indian settlers. These two companion structures were located on the Osage Trace or Texas Road and thus saw a great deal of north–south traffic through the region.

This important road also connected Fort Holmes with Fort Gibson, from where most of its troops and supplies came. By the late 1840s, the California Road passed through the region as well, making Edwards' Trading Post one of the busiest trade establishments in the territory.

A small settlement of Creeks, Seminoles, Delawares, Shawnees and Quapaws grew around Edwards' Store. At the log trading post itself was a cellar that was sometimes used as a jail until outlaws could be transferred to Fort Gibson.

It was to this area that the Dragoons made an expedition in 1834. This regiment of troops had been organized the year before and was under the command of Colonel Henry Dodge. First lieutenant of the regiment was a

The Edwards' Store is a landmark in the National Register of Historic Properties. *Oklahoma Historical Society.*

West Point graduate named Jefferson Davis, later to serve as U.S. secretary of war and president of the Confederacy.

The Dragoons had marched out of Jefferson Barracks, Missouri, to Fort Gibson, where they were stationed. From Fort Gibson, these mounted soldiers proceeded to travel the Plains for the purpose of making contact with many of the tribes in the region who, until this point, had made no treaties with the United States.

The expedition proved difficult for the Dragoons. By the time they arrived at Fort Holmes, many of the soldiers had taken ill. Unused to the heat and diseases prevalent in the region, the regiment suffered high casualties, including Colonel Henry Leavenworth.

Despite these losses, however, the Dragoons continued their march across the prairie and succeeded in convincing several Plains tribes to send representatives to Fort Gibson for treaty talks. In 1835, treaties were completed at both Fort Gibson and Fort Holmes with tribes such as the Comanches and Wichitas.

A young Cherokee who worked at Edwards' Trading Post was named Jesse Chisholm. He married Edwards's daughter Eliza before moving on to establish his own trading post. Chisholm, a multilingual trader, was on good terms with all the tribes in the area, and it is for him that the famed cattle trail—the Chisholm Trail—is named.

MACARONI BOSSES BROUGHT FLAVOR OF ITALY

Brothers Joseph and John Fassino immigrated to America from Italy in the 1880s. Joseph Fassino arrived first to New York in 1886 but shortly moved to Illinois, where he worked in the coal mining industry. He was joined there by his younger brother the following year. They worked hard and saved their money, planning to buy a farm.

But they missed the foods of their homeland and knew other Italian immigrants did as well. So they decided to open a grocery store offering the kinds of pastas and cheeses they remembered fondly from childhood.

They had heard that many Italian immigrants were settling in the Choctaw Nation of Indian Territory to work in the coal mines near McAlester. So the brothers traveled to the little town of Krebs and opened their grocery there in 1892.

As the first store of its kind—specializing in Italian items—the store did well despite the fact that the Italians working in the coal mines were required to shop at the company store. The Fassino brothers got around this edict by smuggling goods into the mining camps.

Joe Fassino gained the trust of his countrymen, and his store also served as a bank for the miners, keeping their savings in a big vault. As the store continued to prosper and grow, Fassino also exchanged currency into U.S. dollars and created passports for immigrants who needed them.

In 1895, a federal court was established in nearby South McAlester, and this brought a surge of new residents and a construction boom. The Fassino brothers opened the McAlester Macaroni Factory in the town in 1897, quickly growing the enterprise to supply pasta to the surrounding states as well as the Twin Territories. The factory, a brick three-story building, dominated the growing business district.

The brothers became prosperous, well-respected leaders in the multiethnic town. Acting as *padrones* (akin to godfathers), Joe and John kept the immigrant communities organized, helping them to solve problems, find jobs and navigate life in a new country. The Fassino brothers helped to preserve the flavor of Italy in the midst of a western town.

MERCHANT SHAPED EARLY TULSA

In 1882, the Atlantic and Pacific Railroad (A&P) would soon merge with the St. Louis and San Francisco (Frisco) line and begin an extension from Vinita southwestward toward the Arkansas River. The A&P had been the first east–west rail line granted access to Indian Territory in 1871. It met the Missouri, Kansas & Texas Railroad at Vinita, a town established by E.C. Boudinot. For over a decade, the A&P had gone no farther than Vinita because of the sparseness of the population in the territory and because of the general animosity toward railroads by the Cherokees. A growth in ranching in the territory made rail lines more financially secure, so an expansion of the line commenced. One of the contractors providing supplies and groceries to the rail workers was a merchant named James Monroe Hall.

Originally from Tennessee, Hall moved to Kansas as a young man and then moved to the McAlester coal field in 1872. At McAlester, he operated a company store for the Osage Coal and Mining Company. When this store closed in 1876, Hall returned to Kansas. He opened a grocery store in Oswego and stayed with it until 1882, when his brother Harry, who worked for the Frisco, gave him the contract to provide supplies and groceries for the rail workers.

Hall moved to Vinita and used a tent to house his moveable store that followed the rail line west. By August, the line had reached the juncture of the Arkansas River with the Cherokee Nation. The Frisco had planned to build a depot at this location. But more favorable conditions in the Creek Nation just a few miles west persuaded the railroad surveyors to move the site. The Frisco Depot was built in the Creek Nation near a settlement known as Tulsey Town. Here, the Hall brothers set up their tent store, choosing not to continue moving west with the railroad.

Other businesses quickly set up their own tents to be near the rail line. The Halls, however, had the distinction of building the first frame structure at a location that is now First and Main south of the railroad tracks. J.M.

This 1890 photo shows the Hall Store, which established downtown Tulsa. *Oklahoma Historical Society.*

Hall helped to lay out the streets for the town that soon became known as Tulsa. He quickly expanded the store, adding a second story and a wide porch to the wooden building. In time, this was replaced with a brick structure known as the Hall Building.

Hall was a faithful Presbyterian with an interest in developing both religious and educational facilities in Tulsa. He invited Reverend Robert Loughridge, a longtime missionary in Indian Territory, to preach the first known sermon in Tulsa to an audience gathered on the porch of his store. In 1884, Hall sponsored a private school financed and staffed by Presbyterian missionaries. One of those mission workers was Jenny Strickland, whom Hall married a few years later.

In 1885, Hall succeeded Josiah Perryman, a Creek rancher, as postmaster for Tulsa, and the post office was located in his store. He organized the First Presbyterian Church, where he served as Sunday school superintendent for forty years. In its first years, the church also met at the Hall Mercantile.

Harry Hall died in 1906, and J.M. sold the store in 1908 to pursue his banking interests. He had organized the Tulsa Banking Company in 1895 and worked as a director of First National Bank for many years. Hall was a great Tulsa booster, organizing a Commercial Club in 1902. He helped to bring Henry Kendall College to Tulsa in 1907 and served as a director well after the school changed its name to the University of Tulsa.

Hall built a nice home for himself and his family on Admiral Boulevard, and it was there that he died in 1935. He is buried in Rose Hill Cemetery.

NICKS WAS GIBSON'S FIRST SUTLER

John Nicks was born during the American Revolution in 1781 in North Carolina. Little is known of his early life except that he received a better-than-average education. He entered the army in 1808 at the age of twenty-seven and saw distinguished service during the War of 1812.

Like so many young soldiers who were mustered out of the army after that war, he continued to live on the frontier, but Nicks chose to reapply for service. He was assigned to the Seventh Infantry and rose to the rank of lieutenant colonel by 1819 before he was honorably discharged in 1821.

At that time, Nicks was appointed sutler for the Seventh Infantry, which was then based at Fort Jesup, Louisiana. A sutler operated a general mercantile on a post to provide the soldiers with food, non-military clothing, liquor, toiletries and other sundries.

Nicks followed the Seventh Infantry to the new post of Fort Smith in 1821 and continued as sutler for this garrison. He also opened a mercantile in the town of Fort Smith with a partner named John Rogers. Nicks was a shrewd businessman but well liked by his patrons. He was elected to the Arkansas Territorial legislature in 1823.

When the Seventh Infantry moved farther west to establish Fort Gibson, Nicks made the move as well, but he continued to operate his Fort Smith mercantile. Coincidentally, he found another trade partner in the new town of Fort Gibson who was also named John Rogers, and they established a mercantile there. The two partners to Nicks were not related to each other. Both stores were called Nicks and Rogers.

Because Arkansas Territory at that time extended for miles west of Fort Gibson, John Nicks continued to serve in the Arkansas legislature. He was appointed to a commission to find a suitable location for a county seat for Lovely County, which included a good portion of what is northeastern Oklahoma today. The site chosen was on Sallisaw Creek in what is now Sequoyah County and was named Nicksville.

Considered the oldest home in Oklahoma, this may have been built by John Nicks, one of the earliest civilians to settle at Fort Gibson. *Oklahoma Historical Society.*

When a road was completed between Fort Smith and Fort Gibson in 1827, the mail route was extended to Gibson, and Nicks was appointed the first postmaster at the fort. Because he was better educated than many of the frontiersmen and enlisted men around the post, Nicks was involved with much of the treaty making that took place at Fort Gibson in its early years. Many of these treaties bear Nicks's signature as a witness to the transaction.

John Nicks met Sarah Perkins in Fort Smith and married her in 1824. They had two children named Eliza and John Quinton. At Nicks's death from pneumonia in 1831, his wife was allowed to continue to run the sutler store until a new sutler could be appointed. Some say this made Sarah the first woman sutler for the army, but others argue that she was never officially named sutler.

Nicks was buried in the old fort cemetery, and his grave was reinterred in the Fort Gibson National Cemetery after the Civil War. Over the years, his headstone fell into disrepair and was almost lost. Historian Grant Foreman petitioned the military to set a new headstone in place, and this was done in 1932. This stone can be viewed in the Officer's Circle at the National Cemetery today.

STIDHAM HAD LONG INFLUENCE IN CREEK NATION

George Washington Stidham left a lasting mark on the Creek Nation in Indian Territory by his many years of service to his people. He was one of the most influential and well-known men among the Creeks before statehood.

Born to a Scotch-Irish father and Creek mother in Alabama in 1817, Stidham did not learn to speak English until he was twenty years old. His opportunities for education were limited, but he worked to educate himself. Around 1837, Stidham moved to the Creek Nation in Indian Territory, settling in the Choska Bottom area near Haskell.

He mastered English well enough that he went to work for the Creek agent as an interpreter. His knowledge of English was also a reason that Stidham was selected to travel to Washington, D.C., on more than fifteen occasions to represent his tribe and address government officials on matters of concern to the Creeks.

Stidham married twice; his first wife died not many years after their marriage. With her, Stidham had two daughters. While working in Washington, he met his second wife, a Miss Thornsberry of Virginia. They had five children.

Stidham went into the mercantile business in the Creek Agency community near Fern Mountain west of Muskogee and was working in this capacity at the outbreak of the Civil War. Along with most of the tribe, Stidham and his family were forced to flee the territory for the duration of the war. They spent that time living near Texarkana. He was elected chief of the southern Creeks but never conducted business in that capacity.

After the war, Stidham returned to his mercantile business, where he employed James Patterson and John Meagher. He later sold the Fern Mountain business to Patterson, who subsequently moved it to the new community of Muskogee.

Stidham then settled in the Eufaula area and opened another mercantile there. Stidham concentrated his efforts in agriculture and is said to have been the first farmer in Indian Territory to plant wheat and utilize a threshing machine. He also encouraged the planting of this crop among his neighbors.

For nearly all of his adult life, George Stidham was involved in the politics of his tribe. When the Creeks adopted their new constitution in 1867, Stidham was appointed chief justice for the nation. He continued in that office until his death in 1891. He also represented his town of Hichitee in the House of Warriors.

George Stidham also had the distinction of being a charter member of the first Masonic lodge organized in Indian Territory and at his death was a Royal Arch Mason. The town of Stidham in McIntosh County was named for this leader among the Creeks who spent his life working for the betterment of his people.

CHAPTER 12

THE EDUCATORS

FIRST SCHOOL SUPERINTENDENT HAD ENORMOUS JOB

Indian Territory's early schools were a patchwork system set up by the various tribes and by different mission organizations and churches. Schools were segregated from the beginning, often even separating boys and girls.

Schools for Native American students were the first to be established by mission organizations. Some, such as the Union Mission near Mazie, operated as early as the 1820s. By the 1840s, the Five Tribes had established schools for their own tribal members. Mission schools continued to develop throughout Indian Territory at places like Tullahassee, Park Hill, Pine Ridge and Nuyaka.

Following the Civil War, some of these mission schools began to teach the children of freedmen members of the tribes. But schools for children who were not tribal members were scarce at first. As towns began to develop along the rail lines in the 1870s, and more and more settlers moved into Indian Territory, the need for schools for their children became acute.

In some larger towns, subscription schools were started. Parents could pay a "subscription" or tuition for their children to attend. In rural areas, education was often neglected. Children were either schooled at home, walked for miles to the nearest subscription school or received no education at all. Most of the schools were one-room buildings with teachers who themselves had often received only a limited education.

In 1898, with the passage of the Curtis Act, towns in Indian Territory could finally incorporate, elect a city government, raise taxes and establish public services, including schools. The Curtis Act also transferred oversight of Indian Territory schools away from the tribes to the Interior Department. Interior Secretary Ethan Allan Hitchcock appointed John D. Benedict, an educator from Illinois, as superintendent of schools for all of Indian Territory. Benedict arrived in Muskogee in February 1899 to begin the enormous task of bringing Indian Territory schools into a uniform public education system.

While the residents of Indian Territory were proud of the strides they had made in education since the passage of the Curtis Act, Benedict felt there was much room for improvement. However, he met with resistance from the tribes, so he spent his first months in Indian Territory traveling among the nations and getting acquainted with education leaders.

Benedict felt that one of the most effective ways to improve public education in the territory would be to provide better teacher training. Working with Benjamin Coppock, appointed superintendent of Cherokee schools, and Alice Robertson, superintendent of Creek schools, Benedict began summer training courses for teachers.

In the Cherokee Nation, the first teaching course was held at the Cherokee Female Seminary in Tahlequah in June 1900. The summer school brought a noticeable improvement in Cherokee schools, so the following summer, the course was opened to any teacher in the territory who would like to attend. Benedict was especially interested in seeing teachers from the rural subscription schools be able to receive further training.

These teacher training schools continued each summer until Oklahoma became a state in 1907. Then schools passed from federal supervision to the state. The Cherokee Female Seminary had established itself as a teacher training facility and would eventually become Northeastern State University.

TEACHER CONTINUED TRADITION OF STRONG NATIVE WOMEN

At her family's homestead on Blue Creek near Coweta, Lilah Denton Lindsay was born in 1860. Her parents were John Denton, who was Cherokee, and Susan McKellop Denton, who was Creek. Both had been born in Alabama and migrated with their families to Indian Territory.

Susan was a descendant of the Perryman family, who were Creek political leaders and founders of Tulsey Town.

Lilah attended school at the nearby Tullahassee Mission and proved to be an excellent student. She also received an education from her mother, who served as a medicine woman in the Choska Bottoms area. Lilah often accompanied her mother on horseback when she called on sick neighbors.

Because she had excelled at school, Lilah earned a scholarship to a female seminary in Missouri and completed her secondary education there. She then earned a teaching degree from Hillsboro-Highland Institute in Ohio and became the first Creek woman to graduate from college. While at college, she also took a medical course and learned nursing in honor of her mother, who had died when Lilah was just sixteen.

With her teaching degree, Lilah was appointed by the Presbyterian Mission Board to work at Wealaka Mission. This mission had just been established in the Creek Nation to replace Tullahassee Mission after it burned. While teaching at Wealaka, Lilah met Colonel Lee Lindsey, who was living in the little settlement around the mission. He was a stonemason, building contractor and Civil War veteran from Ohio. They were married in 1884.

For a time, the young couple lived in Okmulgee and Lilah taught at a Creek school there at the Muscogee capital. Her husband helped to construct the Creek Council House while they lived there. In 1886, they moved to Tulsa, where Lilah had many relatives. She taught at the Tulsa Mission School for three years. When allotments were made, Lilah took her 160 acres in the Tulsa area. She later donated a part of her property for Riverview School, overlooking the Arkansas River.

The Lindseys sold part of the allotment and used the funds for building several structures in Sulphur. In 1907, they built their own two-story home in Tulsa in an addition that came to be called the Lindsey Addition.

Lilah was very involved in civic enterprises in Tulsa, working on beautification and charity projects. She organized the Tulsa chapter of the Women's Relief Corps, an arm of her husband's Grand Army of the Republic (GAR). She also served as president of the Indian Territory Woman's Christian Temperance Union.

The teacher and civic leader, who followed the native tradition of strong women, was inducted into the Oklahoma Hall of Fame in 1937. She died in 1943, and a Tulsa school later was named in her honor.

WOMAN'S VISION LED TO SCHOOL FOR THE BLIND

Lura Rowland was born in Illinois in 1864 and lost her vision from a high fever at age four. Her family moved to Arkansas, and this enabled Rowland to attend that state's school for the blind.

Rowland proved to be an excellent student and after graduation attended Little Rock University. Attending college in the sighted community proved stressful, and she completed only six months before taking time off to rest.

Rowland then took a teaching position at the Arkansas School for the Blind and there found her calling. She proved to be an excellent teacher and continued at that school for five years.

School for the Blind founder Lura Rowland. *Author collection.*

When Rowland learned that the neighboring Indian Territory did not have a single school for blind students, she decided one needed to be established. With her sixteen-year-old sister, Rowland began to travel the territory to determine the number of blind students in need of a school and search out a possible location for one.

Having no funds and only letters of recommendation, she would need to start her school in an already existing building. She could not afford to build. Finally she found a building she thought might be suitable. With permission from the Cherokee Nation, Rowland secured the old military barracks at Fort Gibson.

Now having a location, she next turned to the task of raising funds. Imagine the courage of this young woman, completely sightless and dependent on her sister Cora, traveling from town to town, speaking to complete strangers about a school that had never been attempted before in Indian Territory.

Rowland spoke to the councils of all Five Tribes to explain her mission. While some were reluctant to support an untried enterprise, others were generous in their giving. In three months, Rowland raised $700 and gathered a board of trustees to help run the International School for the Blind.

With these funds and the assistance of her family, friends and other supporters, the teacher turned her attention to cleaning and repairing the old barracks in readiness for students. The school opened on January 3, 1898.

So many students applied that Rowland had to turn some away due to lack of funds. Rowland and her staff of teachers worked at the school with no salary in those early years of constant struggle for funding.

During its first four years, the school relied solely on donations with no governmental support. The Cherokee and Choctaw Nations provided tuition for students who were tribal members.

One Cherokee student who came to the school first as a volunteer was William Lowery. He had been shot in the eye but retained partial vision. After completing his studies, he remained at the school as part of the staff. In 1902, Rowland and Lowery were married. They had one son, Howard Rowland Lowery.

After statehood, the Oklahoma legislature approved $50,000 for the school's maintenance and brought it under the supervision of the state board of education. It then became the Oklahoma School for the Blind. In 1913, the school moved from the old barracks in Fort Gibson to property east of Muskogee that had been donated by Charles Haskell. Today, the school continues the Lura Rowland Lowery tradition of providing quality education for the blind students of Oklahoma.

SANGO WAS ACCOMPLISHED IN MANY AREAS

In 1899, Muskogee was in its second year of offering public education. But many churches in the community also sponsored schools. That year, the African American Baptist congregations began a new school called Sango Baptist College. It was named for A.G.W. Sango, an African American lawyer and educator. The school was located at Fifth and Howard Streets.

Sango had begun his work as an educator at the Tullahassee Mission School. Originally a school for Creek children, it was converted to a school for Creek freedmen after the Civil War.

Sango held a position of prominence in Muskogee's black community in the early 1900s. Besides directing the Baptist school, he had also served as editor of the *Morning Sun*, an African American newspaper. The *Sun* was the second black-owned newspaper to operate in Muskogee and was part of a rise in such publications around the country at that time. It was only printed for about two years, but other newspapers for the African American community continued for a number of years. Included in that number was the *Muskogee Cimiter*, which was published by Sango's friend and fellow attorney William Twine.

Sango was well known as an eloquent orator. He served as a delegate to a statehood convention held in Muskogee in 1901. The convention was basically a series of debates about whether Indian Territory and Oklahoma Territory should combine to form one state or should seek separate statehood. Sango argued for single statehood.

In 1905, the renowned black educator Booker T. Washington visited Muskogee. A.G.W. Sango, along with W.H. Twine, was among the Muskogeeans who welcomed Washington to the city. Then Sango entertained the director of the Tuskegee Institute in his home that evening. Booker T. Washington spoke at an open-air rally in Muskogee the next day.

The accomplishments of African Americans such as Sango were lauded by Washington in his speech. He urged blacks to pursue an education, work hard and take advantage of the opportunities afforded them. A.G.W. Sango certainly had followed Booker T. Washington's advice.

SEMINARY PRINCIPAL INFLUENCED CHEROKEE NATION

The Cherokee Nation established its Female Seminary in 1851, and the school educated young Cherokee women for several generations. This school would eventually become Northeastern State University in Tahlequah.

The Female Seminary—and its counterpart the Cherokee Male Seminary—was extremely important to the Cherokee Nation, providing education that was among the best in Indian Territory. One reason for the high standard of education was the Female Seminary's longtime principal, Ann Florence Wilson.

Florence Wilson was not Cherokee but was a native of Arkansas. Orphaned as a young child, she had grown up devoted to her studies and had received an excellent education in women's colleges in Arkansas and Tennessee.

She was hired as principal for the Cherokee Female Seminary (CFS) in 1875 and served in that capacity for a quarter of a century until she left the school in 1900. As principal, she had a profound influence on her students, known as the Rosebuds. Her curriculum included foreign languages, English literature, math, science, philosophy, music and the arts.

Wilson insisted on physical education as well and required her students to make a daily three-mile walk. This was likely not a burden, however, because

The first Cherokee Female Seminary burned, and only its columns stand today. *Oklahoma Historical Society.*

the male seminary was but one and a half miles away and surely proved to be an interesting destination for the female students.

Though Wilson was a firm disciplinarian, she was not harsh. She genuinely cared about her students and was known to look the other way when the girls stayed up past curfew or engaged in typical schoolgirl antics. And though her rules forbid contact with the male seminary students, that didn't stop the young men from walking the distance in the evenings to serenade the girls who looked out from their dorm windows. Wilson would make herself comfortable in the hall to monitor their activities, but she kept discreetly out of sight.

Florence never married, and many assumed that she had chosen the life of a spinster. But a student snooping in her room one day opened a trunk and found a wedding dress. Wilson had been engaged to marry while teaching in Russellville, Arkansas, before the Civil War. Her fiancé had been killed at the Battle of Prairie Grove.

Wilson devoted herself to her seminary students for the quarter century she spent at the Cherokee Female Seminary. Under her tutelage, nearly one-third of her students became teachers themselves. She was principal during the administration of seven chiefs of the Cherokee Nation, and all gave Wilson their continued support and respect.

Having produced so many teachers, it is not surprising that the Cherokee Female Seminary gave rise to a teacher's college. For several years, the superintendent of Indian Territory schools held summer courses at CFS for teachers from the territorial schools.

Chapter 13

THE JOURNALISTS

PLUCKY PRINTER REMEMBERED AN OUTLAW SCARE

State Comby came to Muskogee with her mother in 1888. They purchased a small home on the railroad right-of-way and settled in to their new community. State, at age eighteen, wanted to get a job, but there were few positions available for women in those days. However, she had some experience as a printer, so she approached Frank Hubbard, then publisher of the *Muskogee Phoenix*, about a job. At first he dismissed her interest, but she persisted, and after several days, he agreed to give her a tryout. She was still working at the *Phoenix* five years later when it was sold to Mr. Singlet.

While working for the *Phoenix*, Comby was very involved in the community and was caught up in the rumors that were flying around town about the infamous Dalton Gang. One of the most notorious outlaw gangs in that day, the Daltons were said to be planning a raid on Muskogee's First National Bank.

The bank was located in the Severs Block at the corner of Main and Broadway. Directly across Main Street from the bank was the Patterson Mercantile, and across Broadway from it was the Turner Hardware.

Determined to thwart the efforts of the gang, bank officials developed a plan. An alarm system was installed at the bank that would sound at the Patterson and Turner stores. These two civic-minded business owners agreed to have guns in place at their upstairs windows facing the bank. It was hoped that any would-be robbers could be halted in the street before they could make a getaway.

State Comby was shopping at Patterson's when the alarm came. Immediately, the store erupted into pandemonium as store clerks fell over one another trying to get upstairs to their posts at the windows. Shoppers just as eagerly rushed to exit the store, either to be out of the way of gunfire or to get a better view of the action. State was so shocked that she was frozen in place by the counter. Just as quickly as the excitement had broken out, everything became deadly still, as if all of Muskogee was holding its collective breath to see what would happen.

Shortly, a gentleman from the bank hurried across the street and into Patterson's. "Tell the boys that was a false alarm," he said, bringing the event to an anticlimactic close.

It was only then that State realized her strength had drained completely from her. She later described the event as one of the most frightening of her life—despite the fact that nothing actually happened. The Daltons never did appear in Muskogee.

FEISTY REPORTER ATTEMPTED FOUR LAND RUNS

Nanitta Daisey was born in Pennsylvania in 1855 but moved with her family to St. Louis while still a child. At some point in her young life, she lost both her parents and was taken in and educated at the Sisters of the Good Shepherd Convent. After finishing school, Daisey settled in Kentucky and took a job as a teacher.

She later worked as a newspaper reporter and took the pen name of Kentucky Daisey, perhaps to disguise the fact that she was a woman in that male-dominated career field. She gained a reputation for her candid and witty writing and was never known to shy away from interesting, if sometimes dangerous, situations to get a story.

In 1889, the newspapers were all covering the upcoming land opening in Indian Territory. Daisey announced that she planned to take part in this land run and headed west. She secured work as a correspondent for two Texas papers and used her position as a member of the press to enter the area a day before the run, riding the Santa Fe Railroad. However, Captain Arthur MacArthur refused to let her disembark, so she was forced to return to Purcell and wait with everyone else to catch a train on the day of the run.

Legend says that she persuaded the engineer to let her ride on the cowcatcher as the train slowed near Edmond station. Daisey's own account of the day doesn't mention this. She did, however, jump from the train at Edmond, drive a stake to make her claim and fire the pistol she had tucked in her waistband to announce her selection. She was able to reboard the train with the help of a fellow journalist as the caboose rumbled by.

It would seem that Daisey had made the claim simply for the story, as there is no evidence that she proved it or settled on it. She took a job as a teacher in Guthrie and got married but never lost the land run fever. A few years later, Daisey raced on horseback in the Sac and Fox opening in 1891. She was thrown from her horse though and never got a claim.

Then she attempted to slip in early to the Cheyenne-Arapaho lands but was caught and escorted to Fort Reno. Finally, in the 1893 Cherokee Strip land run, she entered legally and reached Perry by train. She homesteaded there for a time. Eventually, she traveled to Chicago, seeking reconciliation with her estranged husband, who had followed a military career. She died in Chicago in 1903, but her fame as a feisty and determined Boomer lives on today.

CREEK POET AUTHORED STATE CONSTITUTION

Alexander Posey was a leader in the Creek Nation and is considered to be one of the greatest Native American poets. He wrote his poetry under the pen name Chinnubbie Harjo, and many newspapers carried his writings. He was born near Eufaula in 1873 just after that town developed along the Katy Railroad. He grew up on a farm and attended Bacone College (then called Indian University) in Muskogee.

Posey served as superintendent of the Creek School at Wealaka and the Eufaula Creek High School. He also was superintendent of public instruction for the entire Creek Nation. For a time, he edited the *Indian Journal* newspaper published in Eufaula.

His letters to the editor from a fictional character named Fus Fixico were reprinted by papers around the world. He wrote in a popular style of the day called "dialect writing," in which he re-created the Creek-English that

Creek poet Alex Posey. *Author collection.*

he heard among the full-blood members of the tribe. Through Fus Fixico, Posey satirized the current political situation in ways that were humorous but pointedly critical of how the tribes were being treated.

Alexander Posey also wrote about the name and origin for the Muscogee people. In 1902, a new town was founded west of Eufaula on a new rail line being built westward out of Fort Smith. The town's name was Spokogee, and according to Posey, this was the original name of his people, predating the name Muscogee. He stated that the meaning of this word is "true blood."

In 1905, Posey was a delegate to the Sequoyah State Convention held at the Hinton Theater in Muskogee. He was elected secretary of the convention and served on the Constitution Committee. Because he was a gifted writer, Posey was selected to write the Sequoyah Constitution, and he produced a thirty-five-thousand-word document that later served as the model for the Oklahoma Constitution.

In 1908, Posey met a tragic end when he drowned in the rain-swollen Canadian River. He was buried in Greenhill Cemetery in Muskogee. His wife later published a collection of his poems, and still later, the Fus Fixico letters were compiled into a book. His beautiful poetry and his life's work in education reflected his pride in his Native American heritage and desire to pass the thoughts of his fellow Creeks to future generations.

TWINE FAMILY SOUGHT OPPORTUNITY IN MUSKOGEE

William Twine was born in Richmond, Kentucky, in 1862. He moved to Texas with his family sometime after the Civil War. There, Twine studied law and was admitted to the Texas bar in 1888. He was the first African American to take the bar exam in Limestone County, Texas.

Twine heard of opportunity in the newly created Oklahoma Territory. Land was being opened to non-Indian settlement through land runs.

Several African Americans had made the first land run in 1889, and they encouraged other blacks to come to this new land of opportunity.

In a covered wagon, William Twine made the second land run on September 22, 1891, that formed Lincoln and Pottawatomie Counties. He claimed a 160-acre homestead. When Twine moved his family to Muskogee is unrecorded, but he was practicing law here in the late 1890s. According to a University of Kentucky website, Twine was the first African American lawyer "to carry a capital case from the U.S. Court (Northern District, Indian Territory) to the U.S. Supreme Court."

Twine vigorously defended blacks in court proceedings and would often sleep in the jailhouse where a client was being held. He was always armed and ready to do whatever necessary to deter lynchings. Twine used his newspaper, the *Cimeter*, to inform the black community of their rights and to encourage them to also be ready to take a stand against possible lynchings. The University of Kentucky records that there was never a lynching in Muskogee County.

Twine also used the *Cimeter* to encourage other blacks to settle in Oklahoma. His and other black-published newspapers advertised lots for sale in many of the fifty historically black towns in Oklahoma. The town of Taft was originally named Twine for William Henry Twine. It was changed

The town of Twine (now Taft) is centered in ranch lands. *Oklahoma Historical Society.*

to Taft in honor of William Howard Taft, who had campaigned against Jim Crow laws in Oklahoma's first election.

Twine's sons followed him in studying law and joined his law practice in Muskogee. Harry and Pliny Twine attended Howard University in Washington, D.C. There they would pick up spending cash singing and playing piano in clubs around the D.C. area. Neither pursued a career in music, but William's granddaughter Linda did.

Linda Twine started playing piano in Muskogee before she was in school. She played for her mother's Lutheran church and her father's AME church. Her mother, Frances Powers Twine, engaged Eleanor Barnwell as piano teacher for Linda. Barnwell recognized Linda's talent and ignored the conventions of segregation. Neither Linda nor her friend Mary Warren ever had to enter Barnwell's home by the back door.

Linda went on to study music at Oklahoma City University and earned her master's at the Manhattan School of Music in New York. She was one of the first women to conduct an orchestra for a Broadway musical.

CHAPTER 14

THE TOWN BUILDERS

BARTLES HELPED BUILD TWO TOWNS

In 1867, a band of Eastern Delawares led by Chief Charles Journeycake was granted citizenship in the Cherokee Nation. They purchased land in Indian Territory in the northern section of the Cherokee Nation and moved there from Kansas.

While living in Kansas, Journeycake's daughter, a young widow named Nannie, met and married Civil War veteran Colonel Jacob Bartles. The son of a telegraph operator, Bartles had moved to Kansas with his family when he was ten and later fought with a Kansas regiment during the war. Jacob, or Jake, as he was called, and Nannie moved to Indian Territory in 1873 and settled near Silver Lake, a small, natural lake on the rolling prairie fed by Turkey Creek.

Bartles built a small trading post on Turkey Creek and did business with the community of Delawares living in the area. A post office was placed in this trading post and given the name Bartlesville in 1874. Jake and Nannie prospered among her people, and they purchased a gristmill from an intermarried Cherokee named Nelson Carr in 1875. The gristmill was located on the Caney River where it made a large bend and provided adequate flowing water to power the mill.

By the late 1870s, wheat was becoming a viable crop in Indian Territory. Bartles modified his mill to process flour. He also added a general store

Jacob Bartles, namesake of Bartlesville. *Oklahoma Historical Society.*

with a residence above. Then he added a boardinghouse, blacksmith shop and livery. With such amenities available, the little community of Bartlesville began to attract other residents, and in 1880, the post office moved from the original trading post to this new and growing town.

Towns such as Bartlesville had no legal mechanism to incorporate and form a municipal government. Public services in most territory towns before 1898 were provided by private citizens who invested their own money. Jacob Bartles is credited with providing his namesake town with an electric plant, a telephone exchange and a water system.

In 1884, some competition arrived in the form of a larger mercantile operated by William Johnstone and George Keeler on the opposite side of the Caney River. More settlers arrived, and for a time there was a south Bartlesville and a north Bartlesville divided by the river. The town was finally incorporated in 1897, and in 1899 the post office moved to the Johnstone-Keeler Store, where a depot for the Atchison, Topeka and Santa Fe Railroad had been built nearby.

Jacob Bartles did not let this slow his entrepreneurial spirit. He opened additional stores in Pawhuska and Nowata. In 1900, he moved his Bartlesville store log by log five miles north to a new community he helped develop called Dewey. There, the Bartles family, which now included his son Joseph, operated a bank and hotel and managed a Fourth of July rodeo that grew to be one of the largest in the nation.

SLEEPER HAD BIG PLANS FOR FALLS CITY

Colonel G.D. "Gid" Sleeper was much in the Muskogee newspapers around the turn of the twentieth century for his ambitious plans. He was apparently an optimistic man of vision who saw great things for the Three Forks region.

His plans did not always work out the way he hoped, but that did not stop him from pushing for improvements.

Sleeper was born in Mississippi, but as a young man, he settled in Carthage, Missouri. According to his daughter in a later interview, Sleeper was lucky at cards and put his winnings into developing the first streetcar line in Carthage. It was a mule-powered line and was profitable, but Sleeper may have gambled his profits away. He was broke when he moved to Wagoner before Oklahoma statehood.

He didn't let his difficult circumstances defeat him, however. In Wagoner, he began to trade in cattle and mules and once again prospered. He eventually married the daughter of a large cattle rancher in the area. In time, he bought the ranch from his in-laws and built a house there for his family.

Sleeper's land must have been in proximity to Falls City (present-day Okay), for Sleeper began to develop plans to help the community grow and prosper. This town took its name (one of several) from the fact that it sat near the falls of the Verdigris River.

In 1908, Sleeper offered one hundred acres of land for an agricultural college. Addressing a letter to Muskogee's Commercial Club, he eloquently described the land he was offering just six miles northeast of Muskogee. It offered rich, fertile land, an abundance of natural gas, an artesian well and plentiful building stone. Unfortunately, nothing ever came of this offer.

Sleeper also proposed Falls City as the location for a state fair. Since the community lay in the heart of cattle country with several stockyards in the area, it would be an ideal location for a fair in the eastern part of the state. And having a meatpacking plant nearby would be a great incentive for people to bring their show animals to the fair. But the state fair did not come to Falls City.

The meatpacking plant was another of Gid Sleeper's ambitious ideas. He proposed building a plant to rival those of Fort Worth, Kansas City and Chicago. He was sure that the Three Forks area offered far better natural facilities than any of these larger cities. He invested a considerable amount of money into this project, employing a builder to raise the sandstone walls. He planned a three-story building using local stone and lumber.

Sleeper predicted the plant would cost a quarter of a million dollars when completed. He expected it to process five hundred cattle and one thousand hogs per day and employ one thousand men. He claimed that his meatpacking business, called the North Muskogee Packing Company, had the backing of ten of Muskogee's wealthiest men. But the building never rose above one story, and it was never used as a meatpacking plant.

Sleeper's building would later be used as a stove manufacturing plant, a plow works and a truck factory. It closed as the Depression began and has stood empty beside the Verdigris River since then.

Even though few of his schemes ever paid off, Sleeper was continually optimistic and opportunistic. He ran a full-page ad in the Wagoner newspaper in 1911 offering lots for sale in North Muskogee (the new name for Falls City). The ad virtually guaranteed that the lots would triple in value in a short time because North Muskogee was about to become a manufacturing hub for northeastern Oklahoma.

Sleeper never lacked vision but apparently had difficulty convincing others to fund his dreams. Perhaps if others had shared his vision, the Three Forks region would have had a very different history.

SPAULDING LEFT HIS NAME ON MUSKOGEE'S LANDSCAPE

Homer Spaulding, for whom Spaulding Park in Muskogee is named, was an early-day businessman who moved to Muskogee from Sulphur Springs, Texas. He profited greatly from the tribal system of land use in Indian Territory. He married a Creek woman, Josephine Callahan, and this gave him access to Creek land. His ranch encompassed nearly forty thousand acres on Cloud Creek between Muskogee and Checotah. His cattle herd numbered each year between sixteen and twenty thousand head in the late 1890s.

Spaulding is said to have been the first person in Muskogee to own an automobile. According to the later remembrances of Tookah Turner, Spaulding's auto was called a White Steamer, possibly one manufactured by the Stanley Motor Carriage Company.

Spaulding was proud of his auto and liked spinning around town to show it off. He once drove it to a picnic being held on the bank of the Arkansas River east of town. When Spaulding prepared to drive home, the car got stuck in reverse and almost landed him in the river. Spaulding had to back the car all the way home.

Homer and Josephine were strong supporters of the Methodist Rock Church and rebuilt the school associated with it after it was destroyed by fire. The school, first called Harrell Institute, was then named Spaulding Institute after its generous benefactors. The street in front of the school was called Spaulding Boulevard. Eventually, the name also would be applied to the park that developed between Spaulding Boulevard, G Street, Okmulgee Avenue and Park Drive.

When Spaulding came to Muskogee in 1884, he went to work at the Patterson Mercantile. Eventually, he established his own store with a partner, W.S. Harsha. Spaulding Mercantile also provided banking services to the cattlemen, farmers and other settlers in the area. At first, they simply allowed people to keep cash in the store safe since lawlessness and theft were all too common in Indian Territory. Then the mercantile began to offer loans, accept deposits and keep records of accounts and make payments for individuals on their own checks. Spaulding even issued his own store currency. It was called scrip, and locals referred to the paper notes as "Spaulding scrip." It was used primarily to purchase goods in the Spaulding store, but other people around town would accept it for payments as well.

Spaulding was a true Muskogee supporter and served as mayor of the community in 1902. He promoted tourism and convention business for the city and later went on to serve as president of the Commercial Club, the organization that became the Chamber of Commerce.

The wealthy businessman applied his civicmindedness to the public's benefit when he built a steel bridge across the Arkansas River between Muskogee and Wagoner Counties in 1910. The piers of the long-gone bridge can still be seen from the current bridge on Highway 69.

YOUNG BRICKLAYER HELPED BUILD TAHLEQUAH AND MUSKOGEE

Henry Vogel came to Indian Territory in 1889 after his marriage to Della Brown in Illinois in 1887. Vogel was an immigrant who, at age ten, came to America with his parents. As a young man, he was apprenticed to a builder in Illinois and learned his craft well.

After Henry and Della married, he began looking for opportunities in building, and he saw those opportunities in Indian Territory. Already having a young family, he settled them in Siloam Springs, Arkansas, and then went looking for work.

He found it in Tahlequah, then a little one-street town of about 750 people but an important community in the Cherokee Nation. The Cherokee Council, under the leadership of Chief Dennis Bushyhead, had just decided

Now called Seminary Hall, the Cherokee Female Seminary is an imposing building on the campus of Northeastern State University. *NSU collection.*

to rebuild the Cherokee Female Seminary, which had burned and been closed in April 1887. Vogel helped lay the bricks for the Female Seminary, a building that still stands as Seminary Hall on Northeastern State University's campus. Vogel stated in his autobiography that the bricks used for Seminary Hall were made from local clay because Tahlequah was too far from the railroad in Muskogee to make importing bricks feasible. Lumber for the building was sawn at the local sawmill.

On his days off, Vogel would catch the mail hack and ride to Siloam Springs to see his family. On several occasions when he missed the hack, he would walk the distance between the two towns.

Vogel came to Muskogee after the seminary was completed in April 1889. Because a new federal court had just opened in Muskogee, there were no rooms in the entire city to be rented. His first few nights in Muskogee were spent sleeping in the hay in a livery barn.

There was plenty of work, however, so he planned to make Muskogee his home. With no housing available, he gained permission from Captain Frederick B. Severs to erect a tent on his property and then traveled to Siloam Springs to bring his family to live in this tent home.

Vogel helped build the First National Bank building, now known as the Severs Block at Main and Broadway. He also worked on the five-story Indianola Building at Third and Broadway. At the time, around 1890, this was the tallest building in Muskogee. Bricks were hoisted to the top floor using a pulley system powered by a horse or mule team. The team would have to pull the rope that raised the building materials all the way across the street to a vacant lot where the Surety Building now stands.

In 1892, Della Vogel gave birth to twins—the first born in Muskogee. They were named Albert and Martha and were quite a novelty at the time. Henry Vogel continued to live in Muskogee until his death around 1951.

Chapter 15

The Oilmen

BARNETT LABELED "WORLD'S RICHEST INDIAN"

One of the great ironies of the allotment system was that many parcels of ground thought to be of lesser value turned out to hold great riches in the form of oil. When a group of Creeks rebelled against the government's efforts to assign them allotments, these members of the Crazy Snake rebellion—the Snakes, as they were called—were given some of these "poor" sections of land.

One such tribal member was Jackson Barnett, who was born in the Three Forks area around 1850. Jackson loved raising dogs and ponies and held a lifelong passion for the outdoors. Unfortunately, he was thrown by a horse as a boy and suffered a head trauma that would limit his mental capacities for the remainder of his life.

Barnett worked for his uncle who operated a ferry on the Arkansas River near Fort Gibson until his family built a cabin for him in the Henryetta area. He spent his days roaming the woods around his little cabin, hunting, fishing and living a simple life. His family left him to himself but made sure he had provisions and firewood in his home.

Jackson Barnett refused to select an allotment of land after the Dawes Commission had enrolled him on the Creek tribal rolls. He was declared legally incompetent to handle his affairs, and a guardian was appointed for him. His allotment was arbitrarily selected for him in Creek County near Cushing. The Indian commissioner gave permission for oil exploration on the land.

In the spring of 1912, the Gypsy Oil Company sent a telegram to the Indian agency informing them that the well drilled on Barnett's property was a gusher, producing fourteen thousand barrels of oil a day. Almost overnight, Jackson Barnett became a millionaire and was called the World's Richest Indian.

Many people tried to take advantage of the simple-minded Barnett, and the Indian agent and his guardian were constantly fighting these efforts. In fact, a Kansas woman named Anna Lowe convinced the seventy-year-old Creek to marry her, and they purchased property in Muskogee for a home. The courts became involved in Barnett's affairs, trying to determine how best to invest and safeguard his riches.

It was announced in the Muskogee newspapers that Barnett would be allowed to make a donation of $550,000 to the American Baptist Mission Society to be used as an endowment for Bacone College and the Murrow Indian Children's Home, which were operated by the mission. At the time, this was the largest endowment received by any college in the state of Oklahoma.

Barnett died in California at age ninety-two and is buried there. The federal court annulled his marriage to Anna Lowe, and she had no claim as an heir. However, literally hundreds of other people claimed to be heirs, and it took the court five years to sort through it all and finally declare who was legally entitled to Barnett's riches.

CREEK OILMAN KNOWN AS "INDIAN TOM"

Thomas Gilcrease is one of the best-known oilmen who benefited from an allotment in the Creek Nation. Though he was born in Louisiana in 1890, he moved with his family to the Creek Nation shortly after his birth, and they settled near Wealaka in what is today south Tulsa County. As a boy, he gained the nickname "Indian Tom."

Wealaka was a tiny community sitting on a bluff over the Arkansas River near Leonard. The town had grown around the Wealaka Mission established by Presbyterian missionaries to provide education to area Creeks. It was also near a ferry operated by Daniel Childers, a Creek lighthorseman. Running through the area was a cattle trail that utilized the ferry.

Gilcrease stands by a sign for his oil company. *Oklahoma Historical Society.*

One incentive for the Gilcrease family to move into Indian Territory was the impending allotments of land to members of the Five Civilized Tribes through the Dawes Commission. Gilcrease's mother, Mary Elizabeth Vowell, was Creek, and that entitled her and her fourteen children to allotments in the Muscogee Nation. Thomas Gilcrease was nine years old when he was enrolled with the Dawes Commission in Muskogee in 1899. He received a 160-acre allotment on the west side of the Arkansas River.

Gilcrease attended a rural Creek school as a boy, but his early education was limited. The school was likely overseen by Alexander Posey when he served as superintendent of Creek Nation schools. Some historic sources credit the Creek scholar and poet as being a strong influence on young Gilcrease, helping him to appreciate both his Native American and western heritage as well as instilling in him a love of nature and the arts.

The allotment that Thomas Gilcrease obtained lay within the huge Glenn Pool oil field, and by the time he was in his teens, he had over thirty oil wells producing on his property. The income from oil production enabled Gilcrease to attend Bacone College, where Posey's influence might also have been felt. Certainly Bacone's importance in the world of Indian art would have had an impact on the young man.

After completing his education, Gilcrease pursued a career in oil exploration and amassed a fortune. This enabled him to pursue his passion for western and Indian art. He purchased collections of western artists such as Remington and Moran but also supported area artists from Bacone College, including Acee Blue Eagle and Woody Crumbo. He developed one of the largest collections of American art by any one individual and established a museum in Tulsa for its display.

At one point, Gilcrease found himself in financial difficulties, which put his museum and art collection in jeopardy. Tulsa citizens stepped in to raise funds to enable the City of Tulsa to acquire the collection. Today, the Gilcrease Museum is operated by the University of Tulsa, a college that had its beginnings in Muskogee.

SUCCESS GAINED ENEMIES AND FRIENDS

Real estate investor Capp Jefferson was born on a farm near Smithville, Texas, in 1877. He crossed the Red River and settled in Oklahoma City at age twenty-two and began to buy and sell real estate in the oil-rich city. Like many blacks from the South who migrated to the Promised Land of the Twin Territories, Jefferson was looking for opportunity he could not find back home.

Jefferson married Sedalia Craig from Neosho, Kansas, and they had six children. For forty years, they were active members of the Mount Calvary Baptist Church on Walnut Street.

His investments garnered Jefferson wealth from land sales and also oil and gas leases. But his success brought opposition from both whites and blacks in the city. Jealous blacks called him an "Uncle Tom," and angry whites resented his presence in their neighborhoods.

He purchased a dilapidated home in a predominantly white area and restored the home, intending to sell it. But no one would buy from a black investor, so Capp leased the house to his daughter and her husband, to the consternation of residents nearby. The night before the young couple was to move into the house, it was dynamited.

Such ugliness failed to deter Capp Jefferson. He used his wealth to support projects in the black community, including a Boy Scout camp and a library near Douglass High School. Such benefits for their children changed attitudes, and Oklahoma City blacks heartily supported Jefferson in his two runs for Congress as a Republican candidate. He continually called for racial tolerance and better relations.

Jefferson contributed articles to the *Black Dispatch* newspaper edited by Rosco Dungee; most were about events at his church. He was also a poet and submitted some of his verse to the newspaper as well. His tribute to Booker T. Washington was published as a eulogy for the respected educator. Jefferson moved to Detroit later in life and died there in 1946.

AFRICAN AMERICAN FOUND SUCCESS THROUGH HARD WORK

Joseph Jacob Simmons Jr., sometimes referred to as J.J. Simmons or Jake Simmons, was born near Sawokla, Indian Territory, in 1901. His father, a descendant of Creek freedmen, owned a five-hundred-acre ranch near the town that would eventually be named Haskell.

The elder Simmons, as a member of the Creek tribe, used the Indian system of land ownership to build a prosperous cattle ranch. Jake Simmons, one of ten children, grew up learning the value of hard work by herding cattle and mending fences for his father.

So prosperous was the Simmons ranch that it caught the attention of Booker T. Washington, and the noted educator visited the Simmonses' home while on a trip to Oklahoma. On his visit, he convinced Jake to attend the Tuskegee Institute in Alabama. Washington would become a lifelong friend and mentor to Jake Simmons.

After graduating from Tuskegee in 1919, Jake worked for a time in Detroit but soon returned to Oklahoma. As a member of the Creek tribe, he had been allotted 160 acres of land. In the 1920s, oil was discovered on this land, as it was on much of the land in the Creek Nation. Simmons entered the oil business and became arguably one of the most successful African Americans in the history of the oil industry.

Simmons brokered oil leases in Oklahoma, Arkansas, Texas and Kansas and branched out into real estate, insurance and the cattle business. He worked with other successful oil men such as Frank Phillips and Henry Sinclair. His experience in brokering oil deals in Oklahoma led to his work in representing American oil companies in Africa.

In 1969, Simmons was the first black person to be appointed to the National Petroleum Council. He was also active in the civil rights movement and served as president of the Oklahoma NAACP. He fought for the rights of blacks in the courts but was also a capitalist who believed in creating jobs to help others.

Simmons, who died in 1981, once said, "It is a waste of life for a man to fail to achieve when he has the opportunity." Simmons certainly followed his own philosophy, for he achieved great success in his life of hard work and entrepreneurship.

CHAPTER 16

THE QUEENS AND PRINCESSES

STATEHOOD CEREMONY FEATURED CHEROKEE BRIDE

Shots rang out, church bells sounded and steam whistles bellowed in Guthrie on the morning of November 16, 1907. No longer Guthrie, capital of Oklahoma Territory, the city now was the capital of a brand-new state: Oklahoma! For hours that morning, the early trains had disembarked hundreds of people who had come to the territorial capital to celebrate statehood.

At approximately 10:15 a.m., President Theodore Roosevelt had signed the act of Congress admitting Oklahoma to the Union as the forty-sixth state. With very little ceremony, before a small audience, the president had used an eagle quill pen to apply his signature to the historic document. This event took place in the Cabinet Room of the White House.

Within just a few minutes, a telegram was sent from the White House to Guthrie with the news that Oklahoma was now a state. The secretary to the Oklahoma territorial governor stepped out on the portico of the Carnegie Library, where government officials were gathered, and fired a pistol to alert the city to the news. The new state militia, assembled for the occasion, responded with a volley of its own. And soon there was chaos in the streets as Oklahomans celebrated the momentous occasion.

A large crowd gathers in front of the Carnegie Library in Guthrie for Statehood Day.
Oklahoma Historical Society.

While the mood was jubilant on this day, the same could not be said for the long and sometimes rancorous struggle to get Oklahoma to statehood. Two years earlier in November 1905, Indian Territory citizens had approved a constitution for the State of Sequoyah. Delegates from the Five Civilized Tribes had met in Muskogee to draft the constitution and draw up plans for a separate state. But Congress failed to act on Indian Territory's bid for statehood. Instead, it passed the Enabling Act, requiring the Twin Territories to combine and form one state.

Citizens of Indian Territory accepted this turn of events as graciously as possible but made sure that their candidate for governor was elected. Muskogee's own Charles Haskell was to be sworn in as governor at the Carnegie Library on Statehood Day. But first, a uniquely Oklahoma ceremony took place.

On the steps of the library, a wedding ceremony was conducted, symbolizing the joining of the two territories for life. C.G. Jones of Oklahoma City represented Oklahoma Territory. Claiming to be just eighteen years old (the age of Oklahoma Territory, which had been created in 1890), Jones proposed to Miss Indian Territory. She was actually Anna Bennett, a Cherokee then living in Muskogee.

Anna was born in Tahlequah in 1872 to Thomas and Lucy Trainor and attended the Cherokee Female Seminary. By all accounts, Anna was a very beautiful woman who outlived four husbands. At the time that she said "I do" as Miss Indian Territory, she was married to her second husband, Dr. Leo Bennett. He was serving as U.S. marshal in Muskogee, and the couple was good friends to governor-elect Charles Haskell.

The "bride" in the mock wedding ceremony made her wedding march to the admiration of the crowd gathered around the platform that had been built in front of Guthrie's Carnegie Library. Unlike later drawings that depict her in beaded buckskin, Anna wore an elaborate Victorian dress of white serge.

She was given away by William Durant, a Choctaw citizen from the city that bears his name. The minister who performed the marriage was Reverend W.H. Dodson, First Baptist pastor from Guthrie. After "tying the knot" and joining the two territories symbolically, Governor Haskell was sworn in at 12:20 p.m. on November 16, 1907.

Anna would reprise her role as Miss Indian Territory twenty-five years later in a reenactment of the wedding ceremony. At Oklahoma's centennial celebration in Guthrie in 2007, another beautiful young woman portrayed Anna as the ceremony was acted out once again.

BLOOMFIELD BLOSSOM BECAME FIRST LADY

One of eight children, Alice Hearrell was born into a large but crowded home in the Chickasaw Nation in 1875. Her first schooling came at home because her father, a blacksmith named J.B. Hearrell, hired a tutor for his children. But when J.B.'s health began to fail, Alice was sent to live with her uncle Douglas Johnston. Her two younger sisters, Ada and Daisy, joined her there a short time later.

Johnston was the superintendent of Bloomfield Academy at the time, and he and his wife had also taken in three orphaned daughters of Jesse Chisholm besides their own two daughters. So Alice continued to live in a house filled with children learning traditional Chickasaw values and skills.

With seven girls in his household, heading a boarding school for Chickasaw girls seems particularly appropriate for Johnston. Alice and the other girls attended Bloomfield, and it had a lasting impact on her life. She learned traditional domestic skills at home but studied science, art, music and literature at Bloomfield.

Graduates of this prestigious school were expected to carry on the tradition of the strong and accomplished Chickasaw woman, and Alice did exactly that. The students at the school were known as the Bloomfield Blossoms.

After graduating from Bloomfield in 1894, Alice taught at a rural school near Mead. Used to a house full of children, Alice proved to be an excellent teacher. Eventually, she joined her uncle on staff at Bloomfield.

In 1897, Johnston completed a large frame home, painted white, with mahogany fireplaces and crystal chandeliers. When he was elected governor of the Chickasaw Nation in 1898, his home became known as the Chickasaw White House.

It fell to Douglas Johnston the task of negotiating an allotment treaty with the Dawes Commission. He also had to navigate the changes brought to Indian Territory by the Curtis Act passed in 1898. Needing the assistance of someone trained in the law, Johnston hired a young attorney named William Murray. The gangly and somewhat socially awkward Murray was nevertheless an astute lawyer and gifted orator who took to politics immediately. He was thrown into the social scene among the wealthy and elite Chickasaws and, at a society gathering, met

The Chickasaw capitol. *Oklahoma Historical Society.*

Alice Hearrell. He was immediately smitten, but it took her longer to warm to the firebrand Murray.

The couple was married at the Johnston home in July 1899. The newspapers reported on the marriage of a "prominent young lawyer to a Chickasaw queen." They settled into a log cabin home and began to grow a large family of their own.

Murray attended the Sequoyah State Convention as a representative of Governor Johnston and gained valuable experience in the task of creating a state government. He would reprise this role at the Oklahoma Constitution Convention in Guthrie the following year.

Murray continued in politics and often received coverage by the national press because of his fiery speeches. Alice was sometimes referred to as an "Indian princess," an appellation that she hated because it was contrived and untrue. She was happy being Mrs. William Murray.

When Murray was elected governor of Oklahoma in 1930, however, she did add another title and became first lady of Oklahoma. Her years of experience in the Chickasaw White House had prepared her for this role, and she was a gracious and accomplished hostess in the governor's mansion.

Alice also had the distinction of being not only the wife of a governor but also the mother of one. Her son Johnston Murray was elected governor of Oklahoma in 1950.

MUSKOGEE PAGEANT QUEEN WAS "INDIAN PRINCESS"

In October 1900, Muskogee selected a "queen" to represent the city in a pageant that was to be held in Fort Smith. The young woman chosen as Muskogee's queen was Ella Monahwee, a Creek tribal member who was perhaps a student or a ward of Alice Robertson, for she was living at her home at the time.

The Muskogee newspapers reported that Miss Monahwee would travel to Fort Smith in a buggy that used rubber wheels. This was apparently quite a novelty in those days when most buggy wheels were made of wood with an iron rim. Alice Robertson was to accompany Miss Monahwee to Fort Smith and act as her chaperone. How Ella fared in the Fort Smith competition is unknown, but a photograph of her shows that she was a beautiful young woman.

Ella was a descendant of a town king or *micco* named Monahwee who had fought at the Battle of Horseshoe Bend against Andrew Jackson in 1814. During the War of 1812, the Creeks living in Alabama and Georgia had sided with the British rather than the Americans who were encroaching on their land. The Creek uprising, referred to as the Red Stick War, was part of the larger conflict with Great Britain in which Andrew Jackson made a name for himself.

Jackson's troops attacked Monahwee's town located on the inner banks of the Tallapoosa River in Alabama. The town was called Tohopeka, and when the battled ended, nearly every Creek warrior, over five hundred men, had been killed. The men had chosen to fight to their death rather than surrender to the American forces. Monahwee managed to escape in the night though he was severely wounded. He, too, gained fame among his tribe for his heroic actions at this battle.

The battle proved to be a turning point in Creek history and led eventually to the tribe's removal to Indian Territory. Monahwee's descendants settled in the new Creek Nation as part of the Upper Creeks who were mostly full-blood members of the tribe. We know little of Ella's parents, but in her photo, she appears to be a full-blood Creek.

Ella Monahwee, who was entered on the Creek tribal rolls by the Dawes Commission, later married a man named Newman Jacobs. They resided in Holdenville, Oklahoma, where they raised four sons named Warren, William, Jess and John.

RODEO QUEEN WAS REAL DEAL

She sat astride a horse for the first time when she was two years old and cried inconsolably when she was lifted off the pony's back. Lucille Mulhall was born for the ranching life, but being born a girl meant she couldn't work in the profession of "cowboy." So the pretty, petite and very feminine young woman became America's first true cowgirl.

Lucy was born in 1885 in St. Louis to Colonel Zach Mulhall and his wife, Agnes. When Lucy was four years old, the family made the land run of 1889 and settled on their claim north of Guthrie. Over time, Colonel Mulhall grew his ranch to include over eighty thousand acres of land in Oklahoma Territory.

By age seven, Lucy was an accomplished rider having a natural balance and grace. She was practicing simple tricks with her pony even at a tender age. She loved the ranch and roamed it freely, learning the ropes from the hands. When she was thirteen, she asked her father if she could have a ranch of her own.

Smiling indulgently, the colonel told her that he would give her a start. Any calf of his that she could rope and brand with her own iron would be hers. He came to regret the offer and made her stop when she had three hundred calves. To his surprise, he learned his daughter was an expert steer roper.

Like many other ranchers of the time, Mulhall held rodeos on his ranch, giving cowboys in the area a chance to show off their skills. It was a side business that could earn money during the quiet months between spring and fall roundups. Still indulging his daughter, Mulhall allowed Lucille to compete in his arena in roping and riding events. The colonel's talented daughter may have given him the idea of forming a Wild West show called Mulhall's Congress of Rough Riders and Ropers.

At one of his rodeos, an auspicious guest who fancied himself a man of the West was in the audience at the Mulhall Ranch. The vice presidential candidate, Teddy Roosevelt, was surprised and then impressed with the fourteen-year-old rodeo queen. Stories told later said he promised Lucille that if she could rope a wolf, he would let her ride in his inaugural parade. She returned to the ranch a few hours later with a wolf in tow. Whether she actually rode in the parade isn't known.

Word of the teen roper and trick rider spread, and Lucille was soon in

Cowgirl Lucille Mulhall. *Author collection.*

demand to perform at rodeos around the territory. The first time she appeared at a rodeo in Guthrie, visitors laid odds that this petite wisp of a girl couldn't really rope a steer. She did. And accounts state that her father made $10,000 taking those bets.

Soon Lucille Mulhall began to travel across the country, performing at Madison Square Garden in New York in 1905. Some sources say it was while in New York that the term "cowgirl" was coined by the press to describe her.

Lucille was a star with the Miller Brothers 101 Ranch Wild West Show. In 1908, she married a cowboy singer who opened her act, but though the marriage produced one son, it did not last long. In 1916, she formed her own rodeo troupe and continued her travels, gaining accolades and fans far and wide. With her favorite horse, Governor, she performed dozens of tricks and could best many men in roping steers. She exhibited the qualities of patience and persistence that outdid brawn most of the time.

In 1922, the "First Lady Steer Roper Champion of the World" retired to her father's ranch back in Oklahoma. Lucille Mulhall lived out the life she loved on the ranch, an authentic American cowgirl.

BELLE STARR WAS QUEEN IN THE SADDLE

So many legends surround Belle Starr, the "bandit queen," that it is often hard to separate the facts from the romanticized fiction that has been told and written about her. It has been suggested that she led a gang of murderers and thieves on a crime spree through Indian Territory, but there is no evidence to support such a charge.

Court records show that in July 1882, Belle and her Cherokee husband, Sam Starr, were arrested for stealing a horse belonging to Pleasant Andrew Crane. The warrant was carried out by L.W. Marks, who was the deputy marshal for the Vinita District of the Cherokee Nation.

In those days, when a deputy marshal set out into Indian Territory to make arrests, he generally would rent a wagon, outfit it with supplies and hire a driver, cook and guards. Then he would cross into the Indian Country with a fistful of warrants and begin the job of locating the wanted outlaws.

Commonly, the marshal would set up camp at a central location, form a posse of local citizens, head out to make arrests and then bring the prisoners back to camp, where they would be guarded and fed. When the marshal had served all the warrants he could, he would then take his group of prisoners back to face their charges in Fort Smith.

After her arrest, Belle proved to be a loud and unruly prisoner. As the only woman among the outlaws, she was not chained as the others were. This would prove to be a mistake.

The prison wagon camped at Muskogee on the way back to Fort Smith. They were stopped at the fairgrounds where the International Indian Fair was held each fall. Belle had been eating supper in her tent with a guard seated outside. A gust of wind blew up the tent flap, revealing the guard with his back to her, his holstered pistol within her reach. In a flash, Belle grabbed the pistol and got off a shot, though it did no harm.

The posse returned to find Belle running through the camp in pursuit of the guard, hoping to secure his key and free all the prisoners. She was quickly recaptured, and for the rest of the journey to Fort Smith she was kept handcuffed.

The fairgrounds were familiar territory for Belle. She had often competed in equestrian events held at the fair. Usually she would be up against Indian women who rode astride. Belle stood out in her velvet riding habits riding sidesaddle. Even so, Belle often won these competitions and was a big draw to visitors who came to see her compete. For the local folks, Belle was better known as a queen in the saddle than a bandit queen.

After her attempted escape, Belle and her husband were convicted of horse theft in Judge Isaac Parker's court and sentenced to serve prison time in Detroit. This was Belle Starr's only conviction. This fact never stopped the stories from being told about her, and for many years, the bandit queen was the most famous woman outlaw of the West.

CHAPTER 17

THE ENTREPRENEURS

CHEROKEE MAN BROUGHT FIRST TELEPHONE LINE

Alexander Graham Bell received his patent for the telephone (at first called a liquid transmitter) in 1876. He brought it to the country's attention at the Centennial Exposition held in Philadelphia that year. But many people saw this new invention as just a fascinating novelty and couldn't conceive of how it would soon impact communications worldwide.

A sixteen-year-old Cherokee named Ed Hicks saw the telephone demonstrated at the St. Louis Exposition in 1884. He, too, was fascinated with this talking instrument and began to study everything he could find on it. He was convinced that he could bring it to the Cherokee Nation.

Convincing others was not so easy. Hicks spent a few years learning about the telephone and talking to others about it. In 1884, the editor of the *Cherokee Advocate*, published in Tahlequah, suggested a telephone line be laid from the Cherokee capital to Fort Gibson. The editors at the Muskogee *Indian Journal* responded that the line ought to come all the way to Muskogee, where the Union Agency was located.

To be able to run the line from Tahlequah to Muskogee, Ed Hicks needed financial backing and the permission of the Cherokee National Council. He was able to convince a number of men to invest in his scheme, including J.B. Stapler of Tahlequah and Clarence Turner of Muskogee. Convincing the Cherokee Council proved more difficult.

Viewing the telephone as a "white man's invention," the council was hesitant to allow it. So Hicks set up a demonstration for the council members whereby two Cherokees talked to each other by telephone—in the Cherokee language. Seeing that the instrument could "talk Cherokee," the councilors gave their approval.

In the summer of 1886, Ed Hicks began the work with two African American workers, two wagons for the equipment and a team of mules. Using live trees to attach the wire, they spent the summer at the arduous task of stringing copper wire from Tahlequah to Fort Gibson and then on to Muskogee, a distance of about thirty miles. Because the Cherokees would not allow surveying equipment, Hicks had to use dead reckoning to ensure he kept in the right direction. The line reached Fort Gibson on August 6, and the first call was made.

It took several more days to get the wire through thick river cane and then across the Arkansas River. The wire ended at the Turner Hardware Store, where an operator would take phone messages for everyone in town. Within a few years, more telephone companies were formed and telephone line connected many towns in the region.

UNIQUE ARCHITECTURAL TEAM DESIGNED HISTORIC BUILDINGS

Following Muskogee's Great Fire of 1899, much of downtown needed to be rebuilt, and the owners of the destroyed businesses vowed to build "bigger and better" than before. This provided a demand for the services of a new architectural firm that had recently set up business in Muskogee. The office of McKibban & McKibban, Architects, was located in the Old Homestead Building, and this new architectural team was the talk of the town.

McKibban & McKibban had for the last ten years worked throughout the South, designing both public buildings such as churches and schools and also residences. The firm had provided the plans for the Theological Seminary of Memphis that had been constructed at a cost of $50,000—a very large sum of money in those days. It had also designed courthouses in Tennessee and Louisiana.

Elmer McKibban was originally from Kansas City, Missouri, and was the son of a prominent builder. He had attended architectural school in New York, where he met his wife, Jennie Woodruff, in 1889. They married and

Maddin Hardware Building in downtown Muskogee. *Author collection.*

went into business together as McKibban & McKibban. Jennie was also an architect and had for a time taught at architectural schools. She had, in fact, been Elmer's teacher. A husband-and-wife architectural team was unusual for that day, and their arrival in Muskogee brought them plenty of attention and plenty of business.

One of the buildings they designed in 1899 was for the Maddin Hardware Company. William A. Maddin himself was a prominent builder in Indian Territory, having built the homes of such notable Muskogeeans as Tams Bixby, chairman of the Dawes Commission, and Pleasant Porter, chief of the Creek Nation. Maddin also built schools for the Creek and Seminole Nations.

William Maddin was the Lowe's or Home Depot of his day. Out of his construction business grew several related enterprises, including the Maddin Hardware, Furniture and General Supply Store; the Maddin Lumber Company; the Maddin Planing Mill; and the Maddin Tin and Sheet Metal Plant. It was said that you could contract for your home to be built by Maddin and completely furnish it from his various stores.

It was the General Supply Store that had burned in the 1899 fire. Maddin turned to McKibban & McKibban for the design of a new store to be built next to his planing mill at the northeast corner of Main and Court Streets. This three-story brick building would not only house the Maddin Hardware Store but would also include space for additional stores and offices.

It was completed in 1900 at a cost of $40,000 and was considered a very modern and stylish addition to the downtown Muskogee business district. Besides the Maddin Building, the McKibbans designed a number of business and residential structures in Muskogee and around Indian Territory.

PHOTOGRAPHERS CHRONICLED EARLY LIFE IN INDIAN TERRITORY

While the invention of photography dates to the early 1800s, it is safe to say that few, if any, cameras were in Indian Territory before the Civil War. Life among the Native Americans on the frontier was chronicled by artists such as George Catlin. Early visitors sometimes made sketches of their visits for mapping and scientific study. But few photographs would record Indian Territory until after the railroad began to bring many new people into the region.

One of the first photographers to arrive was a man named J.F. Standiford. A West Virginian by birth, Standiford came to Indian Territory in 1878 after working in Illinois and Kansas. He paid the permit required by the Creek Nation to operate a business in Muskogee and built his home and photography studio. For many years, he was advertised as the only "licensed" photographer in Indian Territory.

In those days, photographers were like traveling salesmen. They did not wait for customers to come to their studio to have their portrait made. Carrying their cumbersome equipment with them, these photographers traveled by wagon from farm to farm offering to photograph the family residing there. This was the primary way in which they made their living as photographers.

Standiford enjoyed travel, so he covered most of Indian Territory looking for work. He was a prolific artist, and many of his photographs survive to this day. A Standiford photograph is often printed on very thick card stock with a decorative border framing the picture. Often, Standiford would identify his photos as having been taken in "The Beautiful Indian Territory."

Standiford's wife and sister assisted him in his photography business, handling the chore of developing the negatives. The photographer had invented a revolving printing mechanism for his darkroom, said to be one of a kind. He also invented an "electric retouching apparatus," for which he took out a patent.

A typical portrait by J.F. Standiford of the beautiful Anna Bennett. *Author collection.*

Other photography studios were established in Muskogee in later years. Alice Robertson ran a studio, and this business is credited with many photographs taken in Muskogee around the time of statehood. An African American photographer named A.P. Greene also had a studio on Second Street in Muskogee. He was best known for his portraits, and some beautiful examples of his work survive today.

Without the work of these early day photographers, our understanding of the past would be greatly diminished. The record of the life of our ancestors creates a connection to the past that continues to fascinate us today.

THE *LUCY WALKER* MADE STEAMBOAT HISTORY

Before the Civil War, steamboats were a primary mode of transportation along the Mississippi River and its tributaries such as the Arkansas. For many steamboats, Webbers Falls was as far as they were able to travel upriver because of the waterfall located there. Webbers Falls became a steamboat landing, and many of the first steamers on the Arkansas paid a call to this community.

One resident of Webbers Falls was a wealthy Cherokee named Joseph Vann. His nickname was "Rich Joe" Vann to distinguish him from a cousin also named Joseph. Vann built a large plantation home near Webbers Falls and raised cotton there with slave labor. The house was a duplication of his plantation home, Diamond Hill, that had been located at Spring Place, Georgia.

As one of the wealthiest citizens in the Cherokee Nation, Vann could indulge his fascinations, and two things captured his interest: racehorses and steamboats. Vann purchased a filly named Lucy Walker, which won many races in the quarter mile. Her colts brought top dollar when Vann sold them and helped add to his wealth.

When he purchased a steamboat in 1843, he named it the *Lucy Walker* after his prize-winning racehorse. Some of the first passengers on the *Lucy Walker* were Seminoles being transported from Florida to their new homes in Indian Territory.

The crew of the boat was made up of slaves from Vann's plantation. He used the steamer to ship cotton from his plantation at Webbers Falls, as well as shipping goods in and out of Indian Territory. Vann was proud of his steamer because it was fast like the racehorse it was named for. In the heyday of the steamboat, captains often tried to break speed records in their travels between river ports. Races between steamboats were also popular, though they often could be dangerous.

In late October 1844, Joe Vann was aboard his steamboat and acting as its captain on a run between Louisville, Kentucky, and New Orleans. Various accounts of this fateful day conflict with one another, so we may never know exactly what happened. Vann's own grandson reported to historian Grant Foreman that the *Lucy Walker* was in a race with another steamboat near New Albany, Indiana.

According to some accounts, Vann ordered the boat's engineer, a slave named Jim Vann, to build steam in the boat's boilers by tossing in slabs of meat. The engineer argued that the boilers would not handle more steam, but Vann threatened him if he didn't comply. So Jim threw a slab of bacon into one boiler and then wisely headed for the stern and jumped overboard.

The *Lucy Walker*'s boiler exploded, killing nearly one hundred passengers. Then the boat quickly sank. Rich Joe Vann did not survive the explosion, but Jim Vann did. Following the Civil War, he settled at Fort Gibson and later told the story of the *Lucy Walker* to Joe Vann's grandson. The disaster was not the worst steamboat accident to occur, but it was one of the most deadly and became a part of the history and legend of steamboat travel in early America.

CHAPTER 18

THE POLITICIANS

EARLY CONGRESSMAN DEFENDED VOTING RIGHTS

Charles Creager was born in Dayton, Ohio, in 1873, and after graduating from Northern Indiana University, he went into the newspaper business. When the Spanish-American War broke out, he joined the Fourth Ohio Volunteer Infantry, holding the rank of sergeant major. His unit was sent to Puerto Rico in 1898, and Creager wrote press reports for his newspaper, the *Press Post*, back home in Ohio. The Colt revolver he was issued during his military service became one of his prized possessions.

Creager moved to Muskogee in November 1904. He was a supervisor of field clerks in the Indian Service in connection with the work of the Dawes Commission. Creager must have liked what he found in Muskogee because he spent the next sixty years of his life there as a vital member of his adopted community.

In 1908, Creager ran for Congress as a Republican in the Third District (now the Second District), and to the surprise of many, he won in the predominantly Democratic area. He was the first Republican to be elected to Congress from Oklahoma and the first Muskogeean to hold that office.

In later years, his widow, Elizabeth, told a story about Creager's campaign for Congress in 1908. He was apparently visiting a gun club somewhere in the Third District and the members were demonstrating their marksmanship skills. Creager was handed a revolver to try his hand at the targets. He bested every club member present—and got their vote!

In those days, carrying a handgun was still commonplace, and Creager was known to keep his favored Colt revolver with him even while campaigning. On election day, he received word that a polling place was denying blacks their right to vote. Creager called a newspaper publisher to go to the poll with him, and while talking to the election workers, he casually allowed the revolver's handle to show. No one was denied a vote after that.

Creager only served one term in Congress, but he used his time there to help build Muskogee. His greatest accomplishment was obtaining the funds to erect the federal building at Fifth and Okmulgee Avenue, bringing in thousands of dollars and hundreds of jobs to the city. Creager is also credited with enabling the city to purchase the old federal jail for one dollar.

Following his one term in Congress, Creager continued to live in Muskogee, working as a teacher, writer, newspaper editor and oil investor. He died in Muskogee's VA Hospital in 1964 at the age of ninety.

FERGUSON WAS LONGEST-SERVING TERRITORIAL GOVERNOR

Thomas Ferguson served as Oklahoma Territory's governor from 1901 to 1906. Appointed by President Theodore Roosevelt, Ferguson held the office longer than any of Oklahoma's territorial governors and is considered to have been one of the most successful.

Ferguson was born in Iowa in 1857 but spent most of his young life in Kansas, growing up on a farm there. He attended Emporia State Normal College and paid for his schooling by teaching at various rural schools. He graduated in 1884, taught school for two years and then after additional training was ordained as a Methodist minister.

In 1885, T.B. married Elva Shartel, the daughter of a newspaper editor in Sedan, Kansas. Ferguson wrote articles for this paper and others as he continued his ministerial career. But when Elva's father died in 1890, Ferguson took over management of the newspaper.

The year before, T.B. had made the 1889 land run but did not retain his claim, so he had returned to Kansas. When the Cheyenne-Arapaho lands were opened in 1892, he and Elva moved the family, their household belongings and the printing press to Watonga. They quickly became a part of the tent community. Ferguson produced the *Watonga Republican* newspaper, and Elva was much involved in civic affairs, helping to establish the first library.

The Thomas Ferguson House in Watonga. *Oklahoma Historical Society.*

From the time of the establishment of Oklahoma Territory in 1890 until 1901, there were eight territorial governors who came and went in quick succession. Legend says that when President Roosevelt was considering appointing yet another governor, he asked, "Is there one honest man in the territory I can depend on?" Ferguson came highly recommended and gained the nickname of "Honest Tom."

Ferguson proved to be an effective leader, having a good working relationship with the territorial legislature in Guthrie. As a former teacher, he worked to improve education at every level, and coming from a farm family, he also worked to help the growing farm and ranch industries.

Ferguson believed firmly in Oklahoma statehood and at first pressed for separation from Indian Territory. But as it became clear that the president and Congress would not agree to this, he acceded and pushed for single statehood. Conflict with two territorial delegates to the Congress resulted in Ferguson losing his job as governor. In 1906, Roosevelt appointed Frank Frantz, who served until Oklahoma statehood in 1907.

Ferguson returned to Watonga and continued his work as a newspaper editor until he passed away in 1921.

OWEN HELPED CREATE THE FEDERAL RESERVE

In 1907, the United States experienced a series of bank failures that contributed to a financial panic across the country. This was the same year that Oklahoma became a state and sent Robert L. Owen of Muskogee to Congress as one of its first senators. Owen, who had organized the first bank in Indian Territory—First National Bank of Muscogee—understood the issues that had led to bank failures and worked tirelessly during his eighteen years in the Senate to strengthen the country's financial system.

Born in Lynchburg, Virginia, to Robert Owen, a Scotch-Irish planter, and Narcissa Chisholm, daughter of a Cherokee chief, Owen obtained an excellent education in Virginia, including a master's degree from Washington and Lee University.

He chose to settle in Indian Territory after his graduation and taught school at the Cherokee Male Seminary at Park Hill. While teaching, he continued his own education in law and went into law practice. At age twenty-nine, he was appointed Indian agent for the Union Agency and

Robert Owen stands with other family in front of the home of his mother, Narcissa Owen. *Author collection.*

moved to Muskogee in 1885. It is said that at one time, Owen owned much of the land that today makes up downtown Muskogee.

His home was located at Okmulgee Avenue and Owen Street, which was named for him. The first ballfield where the Civic Center now stands was called Owen Field in its beginnings because it literally was located on Owen's field.

Robert Owen became very involved in the development of his adopted hometown of Muskogee. Besides organizing the first bank, he also served as president of the International Indian Fair, practiced law there and served on Muskogee's Board of Trade.

When the statehood convention was held in Muskogee in 1905, Owen attended as a delegate, and it was Owen who proposed that the state be named Sequoyah.

Owen's leadership in Indian Territory politics made him a natural choice to be one of Oklahoma's first senators. He made national banking policy a priority while serving in Congress, and when the Senate formed a Banking Committee in 1913, Owen was elected chair of that committee. From this position, he pushed tirelessly for passage of the Federal Reserve Act, which, among other things, established the Federal Reserve system that still regulates banking in America today.

MISS ALICE BORN AS PRAIRIE FIRE BURNS

It was January 2, 1854, and the folks at Tullahassee Mission were celebrating New Year's. Since the first day of the year fell on a Sunday that year, the celebration had been postponed until Monday. It would be a day of no classes for the eighty or so students at the school.

William and Ann Eliza Robertson, the directors of the mission, were anticipating the birth of their second child at any time. Their first child, daughter Augusta, looked forward to having a new baby brother or sister.

Excitement broke out at the mission before the day was over. A prairie wildfire began near Tullahassee, and it soon raged through the dry grasses and trees. Nearly every person at the mission was called upon to fight the fire that quickly threatened to engulf the mission compound. Grabbing sacks and rags, they dipped them into the creek or a nearby pond and ran to slap at the flames licking at the dry vegetation and whipped along by the ceaseless Indian Territory wind.

And then, in the midst of the smoke, flames, noise and excitement, Mary Alice Robertson chose that moment to make her entrance into the world. The birth of one of Oklahoma's most prominent women was nearly unnoticed in the struggle to keep the mission from succumbing to the prairie fire.

Alice, or "Miss Alice," as she came to be called, later wrote about her birth from the family stories she had heard. The weary and smoke-covered firefighters returned just in time to hear her first "objection to the world," as she put it.

In 1891, while directing the Minerva Home for Girls in Muskogee, Alice Robertson received an invitation to speak at a conference. A symposium on the American Indian was being held at Mohonk Lake, New York. Miss Alice would share the platform at the conference with a New York politician named Theodore Roosevelt.

Robertson was the only woman invited to address the conference. Her years of work in education in Indian Territory combined with a stint of work at the Bureau of Indian Affairs in Washington had made Alice something of an expert on Indian issues. Roosevelt was impressed with this woman from Indian Territory, and they formed a lasting friendship.

In 1900, Alice wrote to Theodore Roosevelt, vice president–elect at the time, requesting a political favor. She sought the position as U.S. school supervisor for the Creek Nation. She needed the increase in income this job would afford her because she had taken on the responsibility of caring for her elderly mother. She was also caring for a young Creek girl named Susanna.

When Roosevelt was elected president, one of his first appointments was to make Alice Robertson postmaster of Muskogee. She was the first woman to hold this position in a first-class post office. This pay increase enabled her to build a large rock home on Agency Hill called Sawokla.

Roosevelt visited Muskogee in April 1905. Miss Alice surprised the president by stepping onto the platform where he was speaking. He greeted her warmly as an old friend.

Only once do we know of a sharp disagreement between these two friends. Robertson did not share Roosevelt's opinion that the Twin Territories should combine to form one state. Alice wrote to the president, expressing her displeasure that he had taken such a position. The disagreement did not end their friendship, however, and they continued to correspond through the years until Roosevelt's death in 1919, just a year before Robertson entered politics herself.

Alice Robertson took the gavel to preside over the House of Representatives in June 1921. She was the first woman to do so. *Author collection.*

Alice grew up as a poor missionary daughter and never forgot the hard lessons she learned while her parents served and sacrificed to educate the Creeks at Tullahassee. Those lessons helped define her identity, and she used them as her campaign slogan when she ran for Congress in 1920: "I am a Christian. I am a woman. I am a Republican." For Alice, that said everything about who she was and what she stood for.

The little girl who came into the world in the midst of a New Year's firestorm made a mark on Indian Territory and Oklahoma that was much more lasting than the fire that scorched the prairie. As a missionary, teacher, stenographer, businesswoman, college founder and congresswoman, Alice was born and lived in dramatic fashion.

JUDGE SPRINGER BROUGHT LAWS TO THE TWIN TERRITORIES

William Springer was appointed chief justice of the federal court in Muskogee in 1895. Originally from Illinois, Judge Springer had already played a large role in Oklahoma history even before his arrival in Indian Territory.

Springer had served first in the Illinois state legislature and then as a representative in Congress from 1874 to 1895. As an Illinois congressman, Springer chaired the committee on territories, which gave him a better-than-average knowledge of Indian Territory and the rapidly changing conditions there after the Civil War.

Springer had played a role in giving the federal court in western Arkansas jurisdiction over Indian Territory. Judge Isaac Parker then ruled the territory from the bench in Fort Smith until Congress established a federal court in Muskogee in 1889.

Judge Springer also would certainly have been a part of the debate that had raged for many years about opening lands in the territory to non-Indian settlement. About the same time the federal court was being established in Muskogee, Congress voted to open the Oklahoma lands to settlement by means of a land run.

For thirteen months, the Oklahoma district had no government, no laws and no law enforcement except that of the individual communities that had sprung up overnight during the land run. William Springer introduced a bill to Congress in May 1890 called the Organic Act, which organized Oklahoma Territory. This act established seven counties in this newly created territory. Six of the counties make up the central area of Oklahoma today; the seventh county was composed of the entire panhandle.

The Organic Act also extended the laws of Nebraska over this newly created territory. So until a territorial legislature could meet and begin to enact its own laws, Nebraska's laws would be applied to Oklahoma Territory citizens and enforced by county courts and county sheriffs.

This significant congressional act also, for the first time, officially recognized and used the term "Indian Territory" for the eastern half of Oklahoma. Always before, Indian Territory had simply been called "the Indian territory" with no officially declared boundaries as a whole and no laws that applied to the entire territory. The Organic Act extended the laws of Arkansas over Indian Territory. These laws would be enforced not by county courts but by the federal court in Muskogee and by federal marshals who worked for the court.

Thus, by the time William Springer arrived in Muskogee to assume the position of chief justice, he had already had a significant impact on the laws of the Twin Territories. He was appointed to this position by President Cleveland and was regarded as a knowledgeable and capable judge for Indian Territory.

CHAPTER 19

THE SOCIAL ACTIVISTS

BARNARD CRUSADED FOR SOCIAL REFORMS

Catherine "Kate" Barnard may have always seen herself as an orphan. The future social crusader was born in Nebraska in 1875, but her mother died when Kate was very young. Her father, John Barnard, an attorney for the railroad, traveled frequently, so most of the time he left his daughter with relatives or neighbors.

John made the land run in 1889, staking a claim near Newalla. In 1891, Kate joined him there and attended St. Johns Academy. They later moved to Oklahoma City, where Kate earned her teaching certificate and taught at a series of small one-room schools within a few miles of town.

After a few years, Barnard took a clerical course and worked at various jobs, eventually finding a position with the territorial government in Guthrie. This led to an assignment that took her to the St. Louis World's Fair in 1904. She was one of several hostesses at the Oklahoma Territorial Pavilion.

While in St. Louis, Barnard was able to visit a number of exhibits and lectures devoted to the social sciences and social reform. It sparked a passion within her that would direct the course of the remainder of her life. She returned to Oklahoma City to begin work among the poor, orphaned and overworked.

She began raising funds for social assistance programs and became an accomplished public speaker. When the Oklahoma Constitution Convention

Commissioner of Charities Kate Barnard. *Oklahoma Historical Society.*

met in Guthrie in 1906, Barnard was present, pushing for social reform platforms in the constitution. She succeeded in getting the prohibition of child labor and the establishment of the office of commissioner of charities and corrections. Barnard ran for this position in the first state election and won handily despite the fact that women couldn't vote. With this victory, Barnard became one of the first women in U.S. history to be elected to a state office.

As commissioner, Barnard pushed for laws to require compulsory education, regulate child labor and create a juvenile justice system. She investigated the Kansas prison where Oklahoma convicts were housed and found deplorable conditions. She fought to have these prisoners returned to Oklahoma and oversaw construction of a state penitentiary.

Kate was reelected in 1910, again by a wide margin of votes. She continued to oversee private and state social institutions such as orphanages and mental health facilities. She began to fight the system of guardianship for Indian orphaned children—a cause that made her unpopular with the powerful men who had been appointed as guardians and had profited handsomely from the system.

By 1914, the state legislature had turned on Barnard and slashed her department's budget, thus reducing its effectiveness. Kate, long referred to as "our good angel Kate," left office in 1915 but privately continued her campaign for Indian property rights.

The savage attacks against her by those in power took their toll on her health. Eventually, she retired from the public view, fighting a recurrent illness and depression. She died alone in Oklahoma City in 1930. For many years, her name and contribution to Oklahoma's social justice were lost to history, and only in the last few decades has she been recognized for the groundbreaking individual that she was.

CELEBRATED SCHOLAR HAS ROOTS IN RENTIESVILLE

The town of Rentiesville was established by William Rentie in 1905 on the freedman allotment of the Rentie family. It was one of several all-black towns created in the Creek Nation after allotment, and it flourished in the days of segregation. Buck Franklin, a lawyer of Chickasaw and African American heritage, settled his family here, established his legal practice and served as justice of the peace.

His son John Hope Franklin was born in Rentiesville in 1915 and spent the first ten years of his life in this quiet McIntosh County town. Surrounded by this community of color, John had little experience with the injustices of segregation in his early life. But at age seven, an experience would change his perception of the world and set his course in trying to change that world.

The Franklins would often travel to Checotah to do their shopping, and one day in 1922, they flagged a Katy train passing through Rentiesville. Climbing aboard the passenger train, they entered a car that was reserved for whites. John's parents felt very strongly that they must never voluntarily submit to segregation. So Mrs. Franklin, John and his sister took a seat in the car. When the conductor told them they would have to leave the car, Mrs. Franklin refused. So the conductor stopped the train and put them off. They had to walk back to Rentiesville.

John Hope Franklin points to this moment as a pivotal one in his life. He would face other incidences of segregation and racism, but this one stirred the first embers of his determination to stand against prejudice and injustice.

The Franklins moved to Tulsa in 1925 because Buck Franklin found it difficult to make a living in little Rentiesville. John graduated from Booker T. Washington High School as its valedictorian and went on to further his education at Fisk University in Tennessee. He intended to pursue a degree in law and return to Tulsa to join his father's law firm. But a history professor at Fisk stirred another passion in John, and he instead went on to Harvard to get his graduate degree in history.

For his thesis, John turned to a little-studied aspect of American history: the history of African Americans. His research would later lead him to write *From Slavery to Freedom*, a book that sold over three million copies and has been translated into several languages. John Hope Franklin introduced America to black history in a fair and dispassionate work that continues to be honored today.

Franklin also achieved his lifelong goal of striking a blow against segregation. He served on the team of lawyers and scholars who assisted

Attorney Buck Franklin, father of John Hope Franklin. *Author collection.*

Thurgood Marshall in presenting the legal arguments against school segregation in the landmark Supreme Court case *Brown v. the Board of Education.*

Today, Rentiesville native John Hope Franklin is recognized as the most celebrated American historian, having received 105 honorary degrees from colleges and universities around the world.

TEMPERANCE MOVEMENT WORKED FOR MANY REFORMS

The temperance movement in the United States began slowly in the early 1800s but grew dramatically after the Civil War. By 1873, temperance demonstrations were sweeping across the country, led primarily by women who were troubled by a growing abuse of alcohol. In 1874, the Woman's Christian Temperance Union (WCTU) was formed in Ohio and quickly added chapters across the country. The WCTU used education as well as social and political pressure to advance its cause.

In Muskogee, an organizational meeting for a WCTU chapter was held in January 1884. Laura Harsha, wife of rancher and merchant W.S. Harsha, was a leader in organizing the Muskogee chapter. This group

Laura Harsha, a mother of nine, found time to promote causes she believed in. *Author collection.*

hosted a WCTU convention in Muskogee in 1888.

Laura Harsha, a mother of nine children, had been a schoolteacher in Okmulgee, where she met her husband, who then worked at the Turner Mercantile in that town. They later moved to Muskogee, and Harsha took over the Turner Mercantile in partnership with H.B. Spaulding. Laura never lost her interest in education, and she made it a major emphasis for the WCTU chapter in Muskogee.

At the time that the Harshas moved to Muskogee, there were few schools. Harrell Institute was a school for girls, though boys up to age twelve were admitted. Bacone College taught older boys, but it was located so far from town that it made it difficult for many students to get there. That left a serious gap in education for young men in the community, and their lack of educational opportunities led to idleness and a tendency to get into trouble.

Deciding to remedy this situation, the WCTU opened a school for both boys and girls in 1890. The land for the school was donated by Robert Owen, and Clarence Turner gave the organization generous credit terms for the lumber to build the school. A two-story structure was completed and stood in the vicinity of Okmulgee and Cherokee Streets.

Parents who could afford to pay the school's tuition did so, but no student was turned away because of a lack of finances. Leading citizens of Muskogee supported the school with donations that helped pay the salaries of two teachers. The WCTU was always engaged in fundraising activities.

The group held entertainment events and dinners, held contests, operated a booth at the International Indian Fair and even sold ice cream on downtown street corners to raise the needed funds to keep the school going. It also raised money to begin Muskogee's first free public library.

One fundraiser involved bringing the national president of the WCTU, Frances Willard, to Muskogee. She gave a lecture in the evening that brought out a large crowd of Muskogee citizens. The money that was raised enabled the women to retire the school's building debt.

The WCTU school continued until 1898, when Muskogee's first public schools began. The temperance work of the organization continued until the Eighteenth Amendment beginning Prohibition was passed in 1919.

LIBRARIAN ROSE ABOVE DIFFICULT CIRCUMSTANCES

Judith Carter Horton acknowledged in her autobiography that few individuals came from circumstances darker than her own had been. She was born to Joseph and Ann Carter in Wright City, Missouri, in 1866 to a poor family in a poor community. Judith wasn't able to attend school until she was ten years old, and her prospects for much education were limited.

But this young woman was determined to learn, so she left home to find work and to continue her schooling. She was always older than the other students, but that did not deter Judith. She graduated from Oberlin College at age twenty-five in 1891.

She found work as a teacher in Columbus, Kansas, and then in Guthrie, Oklahoma Territory, the following year. There she met and married Daniel Horton, principal at Favor High School, Guthrie's separate school for black students. In 1906, Mrs. Horton organized the Excelsior Club, the first African American women's club in the territory. The group focused on providing assistance to black students. The club's motto was "To glorify God and uplift humanity." To promote cultural enrichment in their community, the club brought to Guthrie such luminaries as the Jubilee Singers of Fisk University and Booker T. Washington.

When her husband was denied service at Guthrie's Carnegie Library, Horton and the Excelsior Club set out to build a library to serve black patrons. She served as librarian for the Excelsior Library for its first eleven years before returning to the classroom. She then taught Latin at Favor High School until her retirement.

In 1910, Horton became a founding member and later served as president of the Oklahoma State Federation of Colored Women's Clubs, an auxiliary of the National Association of Colored Women's Clubs. These clubs worked to educate and provide scholarships for girls. Horton was also a founding member of the Warner Street Congregational Church.

Horton wrote, "I can conceive of no better or surer way to hasten the education and uplift of our people than the establishment of reading rooms, and libraries in every community. When we become a reading people, we will be a thinking people."

Mrs. Horton's exemplary work did not go unnoticed. In 1923, Oklahoma governor John Walton appointed Judith to the board of regents for the State Training School for Negro Boys at Boley and the Institute for Deaf, Blind, and Orphans of the Colored Race at Taft. In the 1943 issue of *The Crisis*, a publication of the NAACP, Horton was profiled as one of four "First Ladies of Colored America."

Horton remained involved and active in her community of Guthrie until she passed from this life in 1936.

Selected Bibliography

Adams, Janus. "The Lady and Her Music." *New Crisis*, March–April 2001

Agnew, Brad. "Arbuckle, Matthew." Encyclopedia of Oklahoma History and Culture. www.okhistory.org.

———. "Sustaining the Cherokees' Lamp of Enlightenment." *Chronicles of Oklahoma* 86, no. 4 (Winter 2009).

Bartlesville Examiner-Enterprise. "The Real Story of Bartles' Dewey Hotel." July 1, 2018.

Bigham, Randy Bryan. "Life's Decor: A Biography of Helen Churchill Candee." www.encyclopedia-titanica.org/lifes-decor-biography-helen-churchill-candee.html.

Boardman, Mark. "A Boomer Sooner Goes South." *True West Magazine*, April 25, 2015.

Bromert, Roger. "Wilson, Ann Florence." Encyclopedia of Oklahoma History and Culture. www.okhistory.org.

Brown, Kenny. "A Progressive from Oklahoma: Senator Robert Latham Owen, Jr." *Chronicles of Oklahoma* 62 (Fall 1984).

Burton, Art T. *Black Gun, Silver Star.* Lincoln: University of Nebraska Press, 2006.

"Capp Jefferson: A Black Man with Some Wealth in 1930s Oklahoma." www.city-data.com/forum/oklahoma-city/2265911.

Collins, Reba, and Bob Burke. *Alice Robertson: Congresswoman from Oklahoma.* Edmond: University of Central Oklahoma, 2001.

Cryer, Amber. "Fassino, Joseph." Encyclopedia of Oklahoma History and Culture. www.okhistory.org.

Day, Beth. *America's First Cowgirl: Lucille Mulhall*. N.p.: Messner, 1955.

Everett, Dianna. "Ferguson, Thomas Benton." Encyclopedia of Oklahoma History and Culture. www.okhistory.org.

———. "Grimes, William." Encyclopedia of Oklahoma History and Culture. www.okhistory.org.

———. "Organic Act (1890)." Encyclopedia of Oklahoma History and Culture. www.okhistory.org.

———. "Robertson, Ann Eliza Worcester." Encyclopedia of Oklahoma History and Culture. www.okhistory.org.

Foreman, Grant. "Captain Boone's Report of Survey of Boundary Line." *Chronicles of Oklahoma* 4, no. 4 (Winter 1926).

———. *Muskogee: Biography of an Oklahoma Town*. Norman: University of Oklahoma Press, 1943.

Foreman, Grant, and Carolyn Foreman. *Fort Gibson: A Brief History*. Muskogee, OK: Hoffman Printing, n.d.

Gilcrease Museum. "Gilcrease Museum History." gilcrease.org/about/history.

Glaser, Sarah. "The First American Cowgirl: Lucille Mulhall." Porter Briggs. porterbriggs.com/lucille-mulhall-the-first-american-cowgirl.

The Great Seminole Nation of Oklahoma. "Seminole Nation Leaders." www.seminolenation-indianterritory.org/leaders.htm.

Harris, Theodore D. "Flipper, Henry Ossian." Encyclopedia of Oklahoma History and Culture. www.okhistory.org.

Henry, Heath C. "Hall, James Monroe." Encyclopedia of Oklahoma History and Culture. www.okhistory.org.

Hoig, Stan. "Daisey, Nanitta." Encyclopedia of Oklahoma History and Culture. www.okhistory.org.

Little-Known Black Librarian Facts. "Judith Carter Horton and Excelsior." littleknownblacklibrarianfacts.blogspot.com/2011/06/judith-carter-horton-and-excelsior.html.

Logan, Jim. "Saint Kate." *Oklahoma Today*, November–December 2012

Lovegrove, Michael W. "Couch, William." Encyclopedia of Oklahoma History and Culture. www.okhistory.org.

Marks, M.L. *Jews Among the Indians*. N.p.: Benison Books, 1992.

May, Jon D. "Bacon Rind." Encyclopedia of Oklahoma History and Culture. www.okhistory.org.

———. "Bartlesville." Encyclopedia of Oklahoma History and Culture. www.okhistory.org.

———. "Chupco, John." Encyclopedia of Oklahoma History and Culture. www.okhistory.org.

———. "Jones, Wilson Nathaniel." Encyclopedia of Oklahoma History and Culture. www.okhistory.org.

McIntosh, Kenneth W. "Harjo, Chitto." Encyclopedia of Oklahoma History and Culture. www.okhistory.org.

McMahan, Liz. *Okay: Where Oklahoma Began*. Wagoner, OK: Liz McMahan, 1989.

Mullins, Jonita. *Glimpses of Our Past*. Muskogee, OK: Candleshine Publishing, 2014.

———. *Life Along the Rivers*. Muskogee, OK: Candleshine Publishing, 2015.

Muskogee Daily Phoenix. "Friend of the Blind Dies." January 1, 1924.

O'Dell, Larry. "Greiffenstein, William." Encyclopedia of Oklahoma History and Culture. www.okhistory.org.

———. "Simmons, Jake, Jr." Encyclopedia of Oklahoma History and Culture. www.okhistory.org.

O'Neal, Bill. "Canton, Frank." Encyclopedia of Oklahoma History and Culture. www.okhistory.org.

Phillips, Mary. "Sisters Were Early Law Enforcement Officers in State." The Oklahoman. newsok.com.

Reese, Linda Williams. "Mary Alice Hearrell Murray: A Chickasaw Girl in Indian Territory." *Chronicles of Oklahoma* 92 no. 4 (Winter 2014–15).

Roach, Joyce Gibson. "Mulhall, Lucille." Encyclopedia of Oklahoma History and Culture. www.okhistory.org.

Samuel, Nancy B. "Cattle Annie." Encyclopedia of Oklahoma History and Culture. www.okhistory.org.

Sarchet, Corb. "An Appreciation: Colonel Joe C. Miller." *Chronicles of Oklahoma* 6, no. 3 (Fall 1928).

Self, Burl E. "Gilcrease, William Thomas." Encyclopedia of Oklahoma History and Culture. www.okhistory.org.

Shuller, Thurman. "McAlester." Encyclopedia of Oklahoma History and Culture. www.okhistory.org.

Stanford Daily. "Chief Bacon Rind, Osage Tribe Head, Dies at Age of 84." March 29, 1932.

Stiefmiller, Helen M. "Horton, Judith." Encyclopedia of Oklahoma History and Culture. www.okhistory.org.

Thoburn, Joseph B., and Muriel H. Wright. *A History of the State and Its People*. New York: Lewis Historical Publishing Company Inc., 1929.

Tulsa Historical Society and Museum. "James Monroe Hall." tulsahistory. org/hall-of-fame/james-monroe-hall.

Uncrowned Community Builders. "Judith Horton." www. uncrownedcommunitybuilders.com/person/judith-horton.

Wagner, Karen. *Bivouac of the Dead*. Muskogee, OK: Karen Wagner, 1992.

West, C.W. *Missions and Missionaries of Indian Territory*. Muskogee, OK: Muscogee Publishing Company, 1990.

———. *Muskogee: From Statehood to Pearl Harbor*. Muskogee, OK: Muscogee Publishing Company, 1976.

———. *Muskogee, I.T.: Queen City of the Southwest*. Muskogee, OK: Muscogee Publishing Company, 1972.

———. *Turning Back the Clock*. Muskogee, OK: Muscogee Publishing Company, n.d.

"William Grant Rogers." *Muskogee and Northeast Oklahoma*. Chicago: S.J. Clarke Publishing, 1922.

Wilson, Linda D. "Candee, Helen." Encyclopedia of Oklahoma History and Culture. www.okhistory.org.

———. "Lindsey, Lilah Denton." Encyclopedia of Oklahoma History and Culture. www.okhistory.org.

Wilson, Raymond. "Geronimo (person)." Encyclopedia of Oklahoma History and Culture. www.okhistory.org.

INDEX

About the Author

Jonita Mullins grew up in the small town of Haskell, Oklahoma. She attended Oklahoma State University, earning a bachelor's degree in English. For several years, Jonita has written a weekly column on history for the *Muskogee Phoenix* newspaper. With the *Phoenix*, she received the Distinguished Editorial Award from the Oklahoma Heritage Association.

Mullins has published three nonfiction histories titled *Haskell: A Centennial Celebration*, *Glimpses of Our Past* and *Life Along the Rivers*. Her book *The Jefferson Highway in Oklahoma* won Best Non-Fiction Book for 2017 from the Oklahoma Writers Federation.

Her first novel trilogy, "The Missions of Indian Territory," recounts the true-life story of Oklahoma's first schoolteacher. Her most recent novel is filled with Cherokee and Creek history and titled *The Marital Scandal*. All of Jonita's books can be purchased at her website: okieheritage.com.

As a passionate preservationist, Mullins is working with the Founders' Place Historical District to restore the home of Congresswoman Alice Robertson. She founded the Bass Reeves Legacy Troupe, which performs at the Bass Reeves Western History Conference each July. Jonita serves on the board of directors for the Oklahoma Historical Society.

Mullins is a frequent speaker to church and civic clubs, schools and libraries, workshops and heritage events. To book her for an event, she can be contacted through her website.

Visit us at
www.historypress.com
··